Mediterranean Diet Cookbook for Beginners 2023-2024

1900 Days Simple & Tasty Foolproof, Budget-Friendly Mediterranean Recipes And 60-DAY MEAL PLAN

Ronald B. Kliebert

CONTENTS

Sides , Salads, And Soups Recipes 5

MEASUREMENT CONVERSIONS

BASIC KITCHEN CONVERSIONS & EQUIVALENTS

DRY MEASUREMENTS CONVERSION CHART

3 TEASPOONS = 1 TABLESPOON = 1/16 CUP

6 TEASPOONS = 2 TABLESPOONS = 1/8 CUP

12 TEASPOONS = 4 TABLESPOONS = 1/4 CUP

24 TEASPOONS = 8 TABLESPOONS = 1/2 CUP

36 TEASPOONS = 12 TABLESPOONS = 3/4 CUP

48 TEASPOONS = 16 TABLESPOONS = 1 CUP

METRIC TO US COOKING CONVER-SIONS

OVEN TEMPERATURES

120 °C = 250 °F

160 °C = 320 °F

180 °C = 350 °F

205 °C = 400 °F

220 °C = 425 °F

LIQUID MEASUREMENTS CONVERSION CHART

8 FLUID OUNCES = 1 CUP = 1/2 PINT = 1/4 QUART

16 FLUID OUNCES = 2 CUPS = 1 PINT = 1/2 QUART

32 FLUID OUNCES = 4 CUPS = 2 PINTS = 1 QUART
1/4 GALLON

128 FLUID OUNCES = 16 CUPS = 8 PINTS = 4 QUARTS = 1 GALLON

BAKING IN GRAMS

1 CUP FLOUR = 140 GRAMS

1 CUP SUGAR = 150 GRAMS

1 CUP POWDERED SUGAR=160 GRAMS

1 CUP HEAVY CREAM = 235 GRAMS

VOLUME

1 MILLILITER=1/5 TEASPOON

5 ML = 1 TEASPOON

15 ML = 1 TABLESPOON

240 ML = 1 CUP OR 8 FLUID OUNCES
1 LITER=34 FL. OUNCES

WEIGHT

1 GRAM = 035 OUNCES

100 GRAMS=3.5 OUNCES

500 GRAMS = 1.1 POUNDS

1 KILOGRAM=35 OUNCES

JS TO METRIC COOKING CONVERSIONS

/5 TSP = 1 ML

TSP=5 ML

TBSP = 15 ML

FL OUNCE = 30 ML

CUP=237 ML

PINT (2 CUPS) = 473 ML

QUART (4 CUPS)=.95 LITER

GALLON (16 CUPS)=3.8LITERS

OZ=28 GRAMS

POUND = 454 GRAMS

BUTTER

CUP BUTTER=2 STICKS = 8 OUNCES = 230 GRAMS=8 TABLESPOONS

WHAT DOES 1 CUP EQUAL

CUP = 8 FLUID OUNCES

CUP = 16 TABLESPOONS

CUP = 48 TEASPOONS

CUP = 1/2 PINT

CUP = 1/4 QUART

CUP = 1/16 GALLON

CUP = 240 ML

BAKING PAN CONVERSIONS

1 CUP ALL-PURPOSE FLOUR=4.5 OZ

1 CUP ROLLED OATS = 3 OZ 1 LARGE EGG = 1.7 OZ

1 CUP BUTTER=8OZ 1 CUP MILK = 8 OZ

1 CUP HEAVY CREAM = 8.4 OZ

1 CUP GRANULATED SUGAR=7.1 OZ

1 CUP PACKED BROWN SUGAR = 7.75 OZ

1 CUP VEGETABLE OIL = 7.7 OZ

1 CUP UNSIFTED POWDERED SUGAR = 4.4 OZ

BAKING PAN CONVERSIONS

9-INCH ROUND CAKE PAN= 12 CUPS

10-INCH TUBE PAN =16 CUPS

11-INCH BUNDT PAN = 12 CUPS

9-INCH SPRINGFORM PAN = 10 CUPS

9 X 5 INCH LOAF PAN=8 CUPS

9-INCH SQUARE PAN=8 CUPS

Spinach Frittata With Roasted Peppers

Servings:4
Cooking Time:30 Minutes
Ingredients:
- 2 tbsp olive oil
- 1 cup roasted peppers, chopped
- ½ cup milk
- 8 eggs
- Salt and black pepper to taste
- 1 tsp oregano, dried
- ½ cup red onions, chopped
- 4 cups baby spinach
- 1 cup goat cheese, crumbled

Directions:
1. Beat the eggs with salt, pepper, and oregano in a bowl. Warm the olive oil in a skillet over medium heat and sauté onions for 3 minutes until soft. Mix in spinach, milk, and goat cheese and pour over the eggs. Cook for 2-3 minutes until the base of the frittata is set. Place in preheated to 360 F oven and bake for 10-15 minutes until the top is golden. Top with roasted peppers.

Nutrition:
- Info Per Serving: Calories: 260;Fat: 5g;Protein: 15g;Carbs: 5g.

Super Cheeses And Mushroom Tart

Servings:4
Cooking Time: 1 Hour 30 Minutes
Ingredients:
- Crust:
- 1¾ cups almond flour
- 1 tablespoon raw honey
- ¾ teaspoon sea salt
- ¼ cup extra-virgin olive oil
- ⅓ cup water
- Filling:
- 2 tablespoons extra-virgin olive oil, divided
- 1 pound white mushrooms, trimmed and sliced thinly
- Sea salt, to taste
- 1 garlic clove, minced
- 2 teaspoons minced fresh thyme
- ¼ cup shredded Mozzarella cheese
- ½ cup grated Parmesan cheese
- 4 ounces part-skim ricotta cheese
- Ground black pepper, to taste
- 2 tablespoons ground basil

Directions:
1. Make the Crust:
2. Preheat the oven to 350°F.
3. Combine the flour, honey, salt and olive oil in large bowl. Stir to mix well. Gently mix in the wate until a smooth dough forms.
4. Drop walnut-size clumps from the dough in th single layer on a tart pan. Press the clumps to coat th bottom of the pan.
5. Bake the crust in the preheated oven for 5 minutes or until firm and browned. Rotate the pa halfway through.
6. Make the Filling:
7. While baking the crust, heat 1 tablespoon of oliv oil in a nonstick skillet over medium-high heat unt shimmering.
8. Add the mushrooms and sprinkle with ½ teaspoo of salt. Sauté for 15 minutes or until tender.
9. Add the garlic and thyme and sauté for 30 second or until fragrant.
10. Make the Tart:
11. Meanwhile, combine the cheeses, salt, groun black pepper, and 1 tablespoon of olive oil in a bow Stir to mix well.
12. Spread the cheese mixture over the crust, then to with the mushroom mixture.
13. Bake in the oven for 20 minutes or until th cheeses are frothy and the tart is heated throug Rotate the pan halfway through the baking time.
14. Remove the tart from the oven. Allow to cool for least 10 minutes, then sprinkle with basil. Slice to serv

Nutrition:
- Info Per Serving: Calories: 530;Fat: 26.6g;Protei 11.7g;Carbs: 63.5g.

Healthy Chia Pudding

Servings:4
Cooking Time: 0 Minutes
Ingredients:
- 4 cups unsweetened almond milk
- ¾ cup chia seeds
- 1 teaspoon ground cinnamon
- Pinch sea salt

Directions:
1. In a medium bowl, whisk together the almond milk, chia seeds, cinnamon, and sea salt until well incorporated.
2. Cover and transfer to the refrigerator to thicken for about 1 hour, or until a pudding-like texture is achieved.
3. Serve chilled.

Nutrition:
- Info Per Serving: Calories: 236;Fat: 9.8g;Protein: 13.1g;Carbs: 24.8g.

Easy Pizza Pockets

Servings:2
Cooking Time: 0 Minutes
Ingredients:
- ½ cup tomato sauce
- ½ teaspoon oregano
- ½ teaspoon garlic powder
- ½ cup chopped black olives
- 2 canned artichoke hearts, drained and chopped
- 2 ounces pepperoni, chopped
- ½ cup shredded Mozzarella cheese
- 1 whole-wheat pita, halved

Directions:
1. In a medium bowl, stir together the tomato sauce, oregano, and garlic powder.
2. Add the olives, artichoke hearts, pepperoni, and cheese. Stir to mix.
3. Spoon the mixture into the pita halves and serve.

Nutrition:
- Info Per Serving: Calories: 375;Fat: 23.5g;Protein: 17.1g;Carbs: 27.1g.

Almond Grits With Honey

Servings:4
Cooking Time:15 Minutes
Ingredients:
- ¼ cup slivered almonds
- ½ cup milk
- ½ tsp almond extract
- ½ cup quick-cooking grits
- ½ tsp ground cinnamon
- ¼ cup honey
- ¼ tsp sea salt

Directions:
1. Bring to a boil the milk, salt, and 1 ½ cups of water in a pot over medium heat. Gradually add in grits, stirring constantly. Lower the heat and simmer for 6 minutes until all the liquid is absorbed. Mix in almond extract and cinnamon and cook for another minute. Ladle into individual bowls, top with almonds and honey, and serve. Enjoy!

Nutrition:
- Info Per Serving: Calories: 131;Fat: 3.8g;Protein: 2.6g;Carbs: 23g.

Mashed Grape Tomato Pizzas

Servings:6
Cooking Time: 20 Minutes
Ingredients:
- 3 cups grape tomatoes, halved
- 1 teaspoon chopped fresh thyme leaves
- 2 garlic cloves, minced
- ¼ teaspoon kosher salt
- ¼ teaspoon freshly ground black pepper
- 1 tablespoon extra-virgin olive oil
- ¾ cup shredded Parmesan cheese
- 6 whole-wheat pita breads

Directions:
1. Preheat the oven to 425°F.
2. Combine the tomatoes, thyme, garlic, salt, ground black pepper, and olive oil in a baking pan.
3. Roast in the preheated oven for 20 minutes. Remove the pan from the oven, mash the tomatoes with a spatula and stir to mix well halfway through the cooking time.
4. Meanwhile, divide and spread the cheese over each pita bread, then place the bread in a separate baking pan and roast in the oven for 5 minutes or until golden brown and the cheese melts.
5. Transfer the pita bread onto a large plate, then top with the roasted mashed tomatoes. Serve immediately.

Nutrition:
- Info Per Serving: Calories: 140;Fat: 5.1g;Protein: 6.2g;Carbs: 16.9g.

Mediterranean Greek Salad Wraps

Servings:4
Cooking Time: 0 Minutes
Ingredients:

- 1½ cups seedless cucumber, peeled and chopped
- 1 cup chopped tomato
- ½ cup finely chopped fresh mint
- ¼ cup diced red onion
- 1 can sliced black olives, drained
- 2 tablespoons extra-virgin olive oil
- 1 tablespoon red wine vinegar
- ¼ teaspoon kosher salt
- ¼ teaspoon freshly ground black pepper
- ½ cup crumbled goat cheese
- 4 whole-wheat flatbread wraps or soft whole-wheat tortillas

Directions:

1. In a large bowl, stir together the cucumber, tomato, mint, onion and olives.
2. In a small bowl, whisk together the oil, vinegar, salt, and pepper. Spread the dressing over the salad. Toss gently to combine.
3. On a clean work surface, lay the wraps. Divide the goat cheese evenly among the wraps. Scoop a quarter of the salad filling down the center of each wrap.
4. Fold up each wrap: Start by folding up the bottom, then fold one side over and fold the other side over the top. Repeat with the remaining wraps.
5. Serve immediately.

Nutrition:

- Info Per Serving: Calories: 225;Fat: 12.0g;Protein: 12.0g;Carbs: 18.0g.

Morning Pizza Frittata

Servings:4
Cooking Time:20 Minutes
Ingredients:

- 2 tbsp butter
- 8 oz pancetta, chopped
- ½ onion, finely chopped
- 1 cup mushrooms, sliced
- 8 large eggs, beaten
- ¼ cup heavy cream
- 1 tsp dried oregano
- ¼ tsp red pepper flakes
- ½ cup mozzarella, shredded

- 8 cherry tomatoes, halved
- 4 black olives, sliced

Directions:

1. Melt the butter in a large skillet over medium heat until. Add the pancetta and cook for 4 minutes until browned. Stir in the onion and mushrooms and cook for 3 more minutes, stirring occasionally, until the veggies are tender. In a bowl, beat the eggs, heavy cream, oregano, and red pepper flakes.
2. Pour over the veggies and pancetta. Cook for about 5-6 minutes until the eggs are set. Spread the mozzarella cheese all over and arrange the cherry tomatoes on top. Place under the preheated broiler for 4-5 minutes. Leave to cool slightly and cut into wedges. Top with sliced olives and serve warm.

Nutrition:

- Info Per Serving: Calories: 595;Fat: 43g;Protein: 38g;Carbs: 14g.

Mushroom & Zucchini Egg Muffins

Servings:4
Cooking Time:20 Minutes
Ingredients:

- 2 tbsp olive oil
- 1 cup Parmesan, grated
- 1 onion, chopped
- 1 cup mushrooms, sliced
- 1 red bell pepper, chopped
- 1 zucchini, chopped
- Salt and black pepper to taste
- 8 eggs, whisked
- 2 tbsp chives, chopped

Directions:

1. Preheat the oven to 360 F. Warm the olive oil in a skillet over medium heat and sauté onion, bell pepper, zucchini, mushrooms, salt, and pepper for 5 minutes until tender. Mix with eggs and season with salt and pepper. Distribute the mixture across muffin cups and top with the Parmesan cheese. Sprinkle with chives and bake for 10 minutes. Serve.

Nutrition:

- Info Per Serving: Calories: 60;Fat: 4g;Protein: 5g;Carbs: 4g.

Roasted Tomato Panini

Servings:2
Cooking Time: 3 Hours 6 Minutes
Ingredients:

2 teaspoons olive oil

4 Roma tomatoes, halved

4 cloves garlic

1 tablespoon Italian seasoning

Sea salt and freshly ground pepper, to taste

4 slices whole-grain bread

4 basil leaves

2 slices fresh Mozzarella cheese

Directions:

1. Preheat the oven to 250°F. Grease a baking pan with olive oil.

2. Place the tomatoes and garlic in the baking pan, then sprinkle with Italian seasoning, salt, and ground pepper. Toss to coat well.

3. Roast in the preheated oven for 3 hours or until the tomatoes are lightly wilted.

4. Preheat the panini press.

5. Make the panini: Place two slices of bread on a clean work surface, then top them with wilted tomatoes. Sprinkle with basil and spread with Mozzarella cheese. Top them with remaining two slices of bread.

6. Cook the panini for 6 minutes or until lightly browned and the cheese melts. Flip the panini halfway through the cooking.

7. Serve immediately.

Nutrition:

Info Per Serving: Calories: 323;Fat: 12.0g;Protein: 7.4g;Carbs: 37.5g.

Spicy Black Bean And Poblano Dippers

Servings:8
Cooking Time: 21 Minutes
Ingredients:

2 tablespoons avocado oil, plus more for brushing the dippers

1 can black beans, drained and rinsed

1 poblano, deseeded and quartered

1 jalapeño, halved and deseeded

½ cup fresh cilantro, leaves and tender stems

1 yellow onion, quartered

2 garlic cloves

1 teaspoon chili powder

1 teaspoon ground cumin

1 teaspoon sea salt

24 organic corn tortillas

Directions:

1. Preheat the oven to 400°F. Line a baking sheet with parchment paper and grease with avocado oil.

2. Combine the remaining ingredients, except for the tortillas, in a food processor, then pulse until chopped finely and the mixture holds together. Make sure not to purée the mixture.

3. Warm the tortillas on the baking sheet in the preheated oven for 1 minute or until softened.

4. Add a tablespoon of the mixture in the middle of each tortilla. Fold one side of the tortillas over the mixture and tuck to roll them up tightly to make the dippers.

5. Arrange the dippers on the baking sheet and brush them with avocado oil. Bake in the oven for 20 minutes or until well browned. Flip the dippers halfway through the cooking time.

6. Serve immediately.

Nutrition:

Info Per Serving: Calories: 388;Fat: 6.5g;Protein: 16.2g;Carbs: 69.6g.

Berry And Nut Parfait

Servings:2
Cooking Time: 0 Minutes
Ingredients:

- 2 cups plain Greek yogurt
- 2 tablespoons honey
- 1 cup fresh raspberries
- 1 cup fresh blueberries
- ½ cup walnut pieces

Directions:

1. In a medium bowl, whisk the yogurt and honey. Spoon into 2 serving bowls.

2. Top each with ½ cup blueberries, ½ cup raspberries, and ¼ cup walnut pieces. Serve immediately.

Nutrition:

- Info Per Serving: Calories: 507;Fat: 23.0g;Protein: 24.1g;Carbs: 57.0g.

Vegetable & Hummus Bowl

Servings:4
Cooking Time:15 Minutes
Ingredients:

- 2 tbsp butter
- 2 tbsp olive oil
- 3 cups green cabbage, shredded
- 3 cups kale, chopped
- 1 lb asparagus, chopped
- ½ cup hummus
- 1 avocado, sliced
- 4 boiled eggs, sliced
- 1 tbsp balsamic vinegar
- 1 garlic clove, minced
- 2 tsp yellow mustard
- Salt and black pepper to taste

Directions:

1. Melt butter in a skillet over medium heat and sauté asparagus for 5 minutes. Mix the olive oil, balsamic vinegar, garlic, yellow mustard, salt, and pepper in a bowl. Spoon the hummus onto the center of a salad bowl and arrange in the asparagus, kale, cabbage, and avocado. Top with the egg slices. Drizzle with the dressing and serve.

Nutrition:

- Info Per Serving: Calories: 392;Fat: 31g;Protein: 14g;Carbs: 22g.

Mini Pork And Cucumber Lettuce Wraps

Servings:12
Cooking Time: 0 Minutes
Ingredients:

- 8 ounces cooked ground pork
- 1 cucumber, diced
- 1 tomato, diced
- 1 red onion, sliced
- 1 ounce low-fat feta cheese, crumbled
- Juice of 1 lemon
- 1 tablespoon extra-virgin olive oil
- Sea salt and freshly ground pepper, to taste
- 12 small, intact iceberg lettuce leaves

Directions:

1. Combine the ground pork, cucumber, tomato, and onion in a large bowl, then scatter with feta cheese. Drizzle with lemon juice and olive oil, and sprinkle with salt and pepper. Toss to mix well.

2. Unfold the small lettuce leaves on a large plate or several small plates, then divide and top with the pork mixture.

3. Wrap and serve immediately.

Nutrition:

- Info Per Serving: Calories: 78;Fat: 5.6g;Protein 5.5g;Carbs: 1.4g.

Avocado Smoothie

Servings:2
Cooking Time: 0 Minutes
Ingredients:

- 1 large avocado
- 1½ cups unsweetened coconut milk
- 2 tablespoons honey

Directions:

1. Place all ingredients in a blender and blend until smooth and creamy. Serve immediately.

Nutrition:

- Info Per Serving: Calories: 686;Fat: 57.6g;Protein 6.2g;Carbs: 35.8g.

Power Green Smoothie

Servings:1
Cooking Time:10 Minutes
Ingredients:

- 1 tbsp extra-virgin olive oil
- 1 avocado, peeled and pitted
- 1 cup milk
- ½ cup watercress
- ½ cup baby spinach leaves
- ½ cucumber, peeled and seeded
- 10 mint leaves, stems removed
- ½ lemon, juiced

Directions:

1. In a blender, mix avocado, milk, baby spinach, watercress, cucumber, olive oil, mint, and lemon juice and blend until smooth and creamy. Add more milk or water to achieve your desired consistency. Serve chilled or at room temperature.

Nutrition:

- Info Per Serving: Calories: 330;Fat: 30.2g;Protein 4g;Carbs: 19g.

Falafel Pita Sandwiches With Yogurt Sauce

Servings:4
Cooking Time:28 Minutes
Ingredients:

- 1 can chickpeas, drained and rinsed
- 2 tbsp olive oil
- ½ cup hummus
- ½ cup panko bread crumbs
- 1 large egg
- 2 tsp dried oregano
- ¼ tsp black pepper
- 1 cucumber, shredded
- 1 cup Greek yogurt
- 1 garlic clove, minced
- 2 pita breads, halved
- 4 thick tomato slices
- 1 lemon, zested

Directions:

1. Mash the chickpeas with a potato masher until coarsely mashed but chunky in a large bowl. Add the hummus, bread crumbs, egg, oregano, lemon zest, and pepper. Stir to combine. Shape the mixture into 4 balls, flatten them to make 6 burgers. Heat the oil in a large skillet over medium heat. Cook the burgers for 10 minutes, turning once.

2. In a small bowl, stir together the shredded cucumber, yogurt, and garlic to make the tzatziki sauce. Toast the pita breads. To assemble the pita sandwiches, lay the pita halves on a work surface. Place a chickpea patty and a tomato slice into each pita, then drizzle with the tzatziki sauce and serve.

Nutrition:

- Info Per Serving: Calories: 308;Fat: 8.2g;Protein: 15g;Carbs: 45g.

Morning Overnight Oats With Raspberries

Servings:2
Cooking Time: 0 Minutes
Ingredients:

- ⅔ cup unsweetened almond milk
- ¼ cup raspberries
- ⅓ cup rolled oats
- 1 teaspoon honey
- ¼ teaspoon turmeric
- ⅛ teaspoon ground cinnamon
- Pinch ground cloves

Directions:

1. Place the almond milk, raspberries, rolled oats, honey, turmeric, cinnamon, and cloves in a mason jar. Cover and shake to combine.

2. Transfer to the refrigerator for at least 8 hours, preferably 24 hours.

3. Serve chilled.

Nutrition:

- Info Per Serving: Calories: 81;Fat: 1.9g;Protein: 2.1g;Carbs: 13.8g.

Tomato Eggs With Fried Potatoes

Servings:2
Cooking Time:20 Minutes
Ingredients:

- 2 tbsp + ½ cup olive oil
- 3 medium tomatoes, puréed
- 1 tbsp fresh tarragon, chopped
- 1 garlic clove, minced
- Salt and black pepper to taste
- 3 potatoes, cubed
- 4 fresh eggs
- 1 tsp fresh oregano, chopped

Directions:

1. Warm 2 tbsp of olive oil in a saucepan over medium heat. Add the garlic and sauté for 1 minute. Pour in the tomatoes, tarragon, salt, and pepper. Reduce the heat and cook for 5-8 minutes or until the sauce is thickened and bubbly.

2. Warm the remaining olive oil in a skillet over medium heat. Fry the potatoes for 5 minutes until crisp and browned on the outside, then cover and reduce heat to low. Steam potatoes until done. Carefully crack the eggs into the tomato sauce.

3. Cook over low heat until the eggs are set in the sauce, about 6 minutes. Remove the potatoes from the pan, drain them on paper towels, and place them in a bowl. Sprinkle with salt and pepper and top with oregano. Carefully remove the eggs with a slotted spoon and place them on a plate with the potatoes. Spoon sauce over and serve.

Nutrition:

- Info Per Serving: Calories: 1146;Fat: 69g;Protein: 26g;Carbs: 45g.

Mushroom And Caramelized Onion Musakhan

Servings:4
Cooking Time: 1 Hour 5 Minutes
Ingredients:
- 2 tablespoons sumac, plus more for sprinkling
- 1 teaspoon ground allspice
- ½ teaspoon ground cardamom
- ½ teaspoon ground cumin
- 3 tablespoons extra-virgin olive oil, divided
- 2 pounds portobello mushroom caps, gills removed, caps halved and sliced ½ inch thick
- 3 medium white onions, coarsely chopped
- ¼ cup water
- Kosher salt, to taste
- 1 whole-wheat Turkish flatbread
- ¼ cup pine nuts
- 1 lemon, wedged

Directions:
1. Preheat the oven to 350°F.
2. Combine 2 tablespoons of sumac, allspice, cardamom, and cumin in a small bowl. Stir to mix well.
3. Heat 2 tablespoons of olive oil in an oven-proof skillet over medium-high heat until shimmering.
4. Add the mushroom to the skillet and sprinkle with half of sumac mixture. Sauté for 8 minutes or until the mushrooms are tender. You may need to work in batches to avoid overcrowding. Transfer the mushrooms to a plate and set side.
5. Heat 1 tablespoon of olive oil in the skillet over medium-high heat until shimmering.
6. Add the onion and sauté for 20 minutes or until caramelized. Sprinkle with remaining sumac mixture, then cook for 1 more minute.
7. Pour in the water and sprinkle with salt. Bring to a simmer.
8. Turn off the heat and put the mushroom back to the skillet.
9. Place the skillet in the preheated oven and bake for 30 minutes.
10. Remove the skillet from the oven and let the mushroom sit for 10 minutes until cooled down.
11. Heat the Turkish flatbread in a baking dish in the oven for 5 minutes or until warmed through.
12. Arrange the bread on a large plate and top with mushrooms, onions, and roasted pine nuts. Squeeze the lemon wedges over and sprinkle with more sumac. Serve immediately.

Nutrition:
- Info Per Serving: Calories: 336;Fat: 18.7g;Protein 11.5g;Carbs: 34.3g.

Ricotta Toast With Strawberries

Servings:2
Cooking Time: 0 Minutes
Ingredients:
- ½ cup crumbled ricotta cheese
- 1 tablespoon honey, plus additional as needed
- Pinch of sea salt, plus additional as needed
- 4 slices of whole-grain bread, toasted
- 1 cup sliced fresh strawberries
- 4 large fresh basil leaves, sliced into thin shreds

Directions:
1. Mix together the cheese, honey, and salt in a small bowl until well incorporated.
2. Taste and add additional salt and honey if needed.
3. Spoon 2 tablespoons of the cheese mixture onto each slice of bread and spread it all over.
4. Sprinkle the sliced strawberry and basil leaves on top before serving.

Nutrition:
- Info Per Serving: Calories: 274;Fat: 7.9g;Protein 15.1g;Carbs: 39.8g.

Scrambled Eggs With Cheese & Pancetta

Servings:4
Cooking Time:1 Hour 15 Minutes
Ingredients:
- 2 tbsp olive oil
- 4 eggs, whisked
- 1 red onion, chopped
- 3 oz pancetta, chopped
- 2 garlic cloves, minced
- 2 oz goat cheese, crumbled
- 1 tbsp basil, chopped
- Salt and black pepper to taste

Directions:
1. Warm half of oil in a skillet over medium heat and sauté onion, pancetta, and garlic for 3 minutes. Add in goat cheese and whisked eggs and cook for 5-6 minutes, stirring often. Season with salt and pepper. Sprinkle with basil and serve.

Nutrition:
- Info Per Serving: Calories: 315;Fat: 25.3g;Protein 18g;Carbs: 4g.

Pistachio Muesli Pots With Pomegranate

Servings:2
Cooking Time:10 Minutes
Ingredients:

- ½ cup old-fashioned oats
- ¼ cup shelled pistachios
- 3 tbsp sesame seeds
- 2 tbsp chia seeds
- ¾ cup milk
- ½ cup Greek yogurt
- 2 tsp honey
- ½ cup pomegranate seeds

Directions:

1. Mix the oats, pistachios, sesame seeds, chia seeds, milk, yogurt, and honey in a medium bowl. Divide the mixture between two mason jars. Top with pomegranate seeds. Cover the jar with lids and place in the refrigerator. Serve.

Nutrition:

- Info Per Serving: Calories: 502;Fat: 24g;Protein: 7g;Carbs: 60g.

Feta & Olive Breakfast

Servings:4
Cooking Time:15 Minutes
Ingredients:

- ¼ cup extra-virgin olive oil
- 4 feta cheese squares
- 3 cups mixed olives, drained
- 3 tbsp lemon juice
- 1 tsp lemon zest
- 1 tsp dried dill
- Pita bread for serving

Directions:

1. In a small bowl, whisk together the olive oil, lemon juice, lemon zest, and dill. Place the feta cheese on a serving plate and add the mixed olives. Pour the dressing all over the feta cheese. Serve with toasted pita bread.

Nutrition:

- Info Per Serving: Calories: 406;Fat: 38.2g;Protein: 7.9g;Carbs: 8g.

Cheese & Mushroom Muffins

Servings:6
Cooking Time:40 Minutes
Ingredients:

- 6 eggs
- Salt and black pepper to taste
- 1 cup Gruyere cheese, grated
- 1 yellow onion, chopped
- 1 cup mushrooms, sliced
- ½ cup green olives, chopped

Directions:

1. Beat the eggs, salt, pepper, Gruyere cheese, onion, mushrooms, and green olives in a bowl. Pour into a silicone muffin tray and bake for 30 minutes at 360 F. Serve warm.

Nutrition:

- Info Per Serving: Calories: 120;Fat: 6g;Protein: 8g;Carbs: 10g.

Basic Tortilla De Patatas

Servings:4
Cooking Time:35 Minutes
Ingredients:

- 1 ½ lb gold potatoes, peeled and sliced
- ½ cup olive oil
- 1 sweet onion, thinly sliced
- 8 eggs
- ½ dried oregano
- Salt to taste

Directions:

1. Heat the olive oil in a skillet over medium heat. Fry the potatoes for 8-10 minutes, stirring often. Add in onion, oregano, and salt and cook for 5-6 minutes until the potatoes are tender and slightly golden; set aside.

2. In a bowl, beat the eggs with a pinch of salt. Add in the potato mixture and mix well. Pour into the skillet and cook for about 10-12 minutes. Flip the tortilla using a plate, and cook for 2 more minutes until nice and crispy. Slice and serve.

Nutrition:

- Info Per Serving: Calories: 440;Fat: 34g;Protein: 14g;Carbs: 22g.

Honey & Feta Frozen Yogurt

Servings:4
Cooking Time:5 Minutes + Freezing Time
Ingredients:

- 1 tbsp honey
- 1 cup Greek yogurt
- ½ cup feta cheese, crumbled
- 2 tbsp mint leaves, chopped

Directions:

1. In a food processor, blend yogurt, honey, and feta cheese until smooth. Transfer to a wide dish, cover with plastic wrap, and put in the freezer for 2 hours or until solid. When frozen, spoon into cups, sprinkle with mint, and serve.

Nutrition:

- Info Per Serving: Calories: 170;Fat: 12g;Protein: 7g;Carbs: 13g.

Avocado And Egg Toast

Servings:2
Cooking Time: 8 Minutes
Ingredients:

- 2 tablespoons ground flaxseed
- ½ teaspoon baking powder
- 2 large eggs, beaten
- 1 teaspoon salt, plus additional for serving
- ½ teaspoon freshly ground black pepper, plus additional for serving
- ½ teaspoon garlic powder, sesame seed, caraway seed, or other dried herbs (optional)
- 3 tablespoons extra-virgin olive oil, divided
- 1 medium ripe avocado, peeled, pitted, and sliced
- 2 tablespoons chopped ripe tomato

Directions:

1. In a small bowl, combine the flaxseed and baking powder, breaking up any lumps in the baking powder.
2. Add the beaten eggs, salt, pepper, and garlic powder (if desired) and whisk well. Let sit for 2 minutes.
3. In a small nonstick skillet, heat 1 tablespoon of olive oil over medium heat. Pour the egg mixture into the skillet and let cook undisturbed until the egg begins to set on bottom, 2 to 3 minutes.
4. Using a rubber spatula, scrape down the sides to allow uncooked egg to reach the bottom. Cook for an additional 2 to 3 minutes.
5. Once almost set, flip like a pancake and allow the top to fully cook, another 1 to 2 minutes.

6. Remove from the skillet and allow to cool slightl then slice into 2 pieces.
7. Top each piece with avocado slices, additional sa and pepper, chopped tomato, and drizzle with th remaining 2 tablespoons of olive oil. Serve immediate

Nutrition:

- Info Per Serving: Calories: 297;Fat: 26.1g;Protei 8.9g;Carbs: 12.0g.

Open-faced Margherita Sandwiches

Servings:4
Cooking Time: 5 Minutes
Ingredients:

- 2 whole-wheat submarine or hoagie rolls, slice open horizontally
- 1 tablespoon extra-virgin olive oil
- 1 garlic clove, halved
- 1 large ripe tomato, cut into 8 slices
- ¼ teaspoon dried oregano
- 1 cup fresh Mozzarella, sliced
- ¼ cup lightly packed fresh basil leaves, torn in small pieces
- ¼ teaspoon freshly ground black pepper

Directions:

1. Preheat the broiler to High with the rack 4 inch under the heating element.
2. Put the sliced bread on a large, rimmed bakir sheet and broil for 1 minute, or until the bread is ju lightly toasted. Remove from the oven.
3. Brush each piece of the toasted bread with the o and rub a garlic half over each piece.
4. Put the toasted bread back on the baking shee Evenly divide the tomato slices on each piece. Sprink with the oregano and top with the cheese.
5. Place the baking sheet under the broiler. Set th timer for 1½ minutes, but check after 1 minute. Whe the cheese is melted and the edges are just starting get dark brown, remove the sandwiches from the over
6. Top each sandwich with the fresh basil and pepp before serving.

Nutrition:

- Info Per Serving: Calories: 93;Fat: 2.0g;Protei 10.0g;Carbs: 8.0g.

Vegetable & Cheese Frittata

Servings:4
Cooking Time:30 Minutes
Ingredients:

- 2 tbsp olive oil
- ½ lb cauliflower florets
- ½ cup skimmed milk
- 6 eggs
- 1 red bell pepper, chopped
- ½ cup fontina cheese, grated
- ½ tsp red pepper
- ½ tsp turmeric
- Salt and black pepper to taste

Directions:

1. Preheat oven to 360 F. In a bowl, beat the eggs with milk. Add in fontina cheese, red pepper, turmeric, salt, and pepper. Mix in red bell pepper. Warm olive oil in a skillet over medium heat, pour in the egg mixture and cook for 4-5 minutes. Set aside.
2. Blanch the cauliflower florets in a pot for 5 minutes until tender. Spread over the egg mixture. Place the skillet in the oven and bake for 15 minutes or until golden brown. Allow cooling for a few minutes before slicing. Serve warm.

Nutrition:

- Info Per Serving: Calories: 312;Fat: 18g;Protein: 21g;Carbs: 17g.

Zucchini & Ricotta Egg Muffins

Servings:4
Cooking Time:20 Minutes
Ingredients:

- 3 tbsp olive oil
- ½ cup ricotta cheese, crumbled
- 1 lb zucchini, spiralized
- ¼ cup sweet onion, chopped
- 4 large eggs
- ½ tsp hot paprika
- 2 tbsp fresh parsley, chopped
- Salt and black pepper to taste

Directions:

1. Preheat oven to 350 F.Combine the zucchini and sweet onion with olive oil, salt, and black pepper in a bowl. Divide between greased muffin cups. Crack an egg in each one; scatter some salt and hot paprika. Bake for 12 minutes or until set. Serve topped with ricotta cheese and parsley.

Nutrition:

- Info Per Serving: Calories: 226;Fat: 4.6g;Protein: 11g;Carbs: 6.6g.

White Pizzas With Arugula And Spinach

Servings:4
Cooking Time: 20 Minutes
Ingredients:

- 1 pound refrigerated fresh pizza dough
- 2 tablespoons extra-virgin olive oil, divided
- ½ cup thinly sliced onion
- 2 garlic cloves, minced
- 3 cups baby spinach
- 3 cups arugula
- 1 tablespoon water
- ¼ teaspoon freshly ground black pepper
- 1 tablespoon freshly squeezed lemon juice
- ½ cup shredded Parmesan cheese
- ½ cup crumbled goat cheese
- Cooking spray

Directions:

1. Preheat the oven to 500ºF. Spritz a large, rimmed baking sheet with cooking spray.
2. Take the pizza dough out of the refrigerator.
3. Heat 1 tablespoon of the oil in a large skillet over medium heat. Add the onion to the skillet and cook for 4 minutes, stirring constantly. Add the garlic and cook for 1 minute, stirring constantly.
4. Stir in the spinach, arugula, water and pepper. Cook for about 2 minutes, stirring constantly, or until all the greens are coated with oil and they start to cook down. Remove the skillet from the heat and drizzle with the lemon juice.
5. On a lightly floured work surface, form the pizza dough into a 12-inch circle or a 10-by-12-inch rectangle, using a rolling pin or by stretching with your hands.
6. Place the dough on the prepared baking sheet. Brush the dough with the remaining 1 tablespoon of the oil. Spread the cooked greens on top of the dough to within ½ inch of the edge. Top with the Parmesan cheese and goat cheese.
7. Bake in the preheated oven for 10 to 12 minutes, or until the crust starts to brown around the edges.
8. Remove from the oven and transfer the pizza to a cutting board. Cut into eight pieces before serving.

Nutrition:

- Info Per Serving: Calories: 521;Fat: 31.0g;Protein: 23.0g;Carbs: 38.0g.

Cheese Egg Quiche

Servings:6
Cooking Time:45 Minutes
Ingredients:

- 1 tbsp melted butter
- 1 ¼ cups crumbled feta
- ½ cup ricotta, crumbled
- 2 tbsp chopped fresh mint
- 1 tbsp chopped fresh dill
- ½ tsp lemon zest
- Black pepper to taste
- 2 large eggs, beaten

Directions:

1. Preheat the oven to 350 F. In a medium bowl, combine the feta and ricotta cheeses and blend them well with a fork. Stir in the mint, dill, lemon zest, and black pepper. Slowly add the eggs to the cheese mixture and blend well. Pour the batter into a greased baking dish and drizzle with melted butter. Bake until lightly browned, 35-40 minutes. Serve.

Nutrition:

- Info Per Serving: Calories: 182;Fat: 17g;Protein: 7g;Carbs: 2g.

Tomato And Egg Scramble

Servings:4
Cooking Time: 20 Minutes
Ingredients:

- 2 tablespoons extra-virgin olive oil
- ¼ cup finely minced red onion
- 1½ cups chopped fresh tomatoes
- 2 garlic cloves, minced
- ½ teaspoon dried thyme
- ½ teaspoon dried oregano
- 8 large eggs
- ½ teaspoon salt
- ¼ teaspoon freshly ground black pepper
- ¾ cup crumbled feta cheese
- ¼ cup chopped fresh mint leaves

Directions:

1. Heat the olive oil in a large skillet over medium heat.

2. Sauté the red onion and tomatoes in the hot skillet for 10 to 12 minutes, or until the tomatoes are softened.

3. Stir in the garlic, thyme, and oregano and sauté for 2 to 4 minutes, or until the garlic is fragrant.

4. Meanwhile, beat the eggs with the salt and pepper in a medium bowl until frothy.

5. Pour the beaten eggs into the skillet and reduce the heat to low. Scramble

6. for 3 to 4 minutes, stirring constantly, or until the eggs are set.

7. Remove from the heat and scatter with the feta cheese and mint. Serve warm.

Nutrition:

- Info Per Serving: Calories: 260;Fat: 21.9g;Protein 10.2g;Carbs: 5.8g.

Basil Cheese Omelet

Servings:2
Cooking Time:20 Minutes
Ingredients:

- 1 tbsp olive oil
- ½ pint cherry tomatoes
- 2 garlic cloves, minced
- 5 large eggs, beaten
- 3 tbsp milk
- Salt and black pepper to taste
- 2 tbsp fresh oregano, minced
- 2 tbsp fresh basil, minced
- 2 oz ricotta cheese, crumbled

Directions:

1. Warm the olive oil in a skillet over medium heat. Add the cherry tomatoes. Reduce the heat, cover the pan, and let the tomatoes soften. When the tomatoes are mostly softened and broken down, remove the lid, add garlic and continue to sauté.

2. In a bowl, combine the eggs, milk, salt, pepper, and herbs and whisk well to combine. Increase the heat to medium, pour the egg mixture over the tomatoes and garlic, and then sprinkle with ricotta cheese. Cook for 7-8 minutes, flipping once until the eggs are set. Run a spatula around the edge of the pan to make sure they won't stick. Serve warm.

Nutrition:

- Info Per Serving: Calories: 394;Fat: 29.6g;Protein 26g;Carbs: 6g.

Apple-oat Porridge With Cranberries

Servings:4
Cooking Time:15 Minutes
Ingredients:

- 3 green apples, cored, peeled and cubed
- 2 cups milk
- ½ cup walnuts, chopped
- 3 tbsp maple syrup
- ½ cup steel cut oats
- ½ tsp cinnamon powder
- ½ cup cranberries, dried
- 1 tsp vanilla extract

Directions:
. Warm the milk in a pot over medium heat and stir in apples, maple syrup, oats, cinnamon powder, cranberries, vanilla extract, and 1 cup water. Simmer for 10 minutes. Ladle the porridge into serving bowls, op with walnuts, and serve.

Nutrition:
Info Per Serving: Calories: 160;Fat: 3g;Protein: g;Carbs: 4g.

Sweet Banana Pancakes With Strawberries

Servings:4
Cooking Time:15 Minutes
Ingredients:

- 2 tbsp olive oil
- 1 cup flour
- 1 cup + 2 tbsp milk
- 2 eggs, beaten
- ⅓ cup honey
- 1 tsp baking soda
- ¼ tsp salt
- 1 sliced banana
- 1 cup sliced strawberries
- 1 tbsp maple syrup

Directions:
. Mix together the flour, milk, eggs, honey, baking oda, and salt in a bowl. Warm the olive oil in a skillet ver medium heat and pour in ⅓ cup of the pancake atter. Cook for 2-3 minutes. Add half of the fresh fruit nd flip to cook for 2-3 minutes on the other side until ooked through. Top with the remaining fruit, drizzle ith maple syrup and serve.

Nutrition:

- Info Per Serving: Calories: 415;Fat: 24g;Protein: 12g;Carbs: 46g.

Poached Egg & Avocado Toasts

Servings:4
Cooking Time:15 Minutes
Ingredients:

- 4 bread slices, toasted
- 4 eggs
- 2 avocados, chopped
- ¼ cup chopped fresh cilantro
- 3 tbsp red wine vinegar
- 1 lemon, juiced and zested
- 1 garlic clove, minced
- Salt and black pepper to taste
- 1 tsp hot sauce

Directions:
1. Puree avocados, cilantro, lemon juice, lemon zest, garlic, 2 tbsp of vinegar, salt, black pepper, and hot sauce with an immersion blender in a bowl until smooth. Bring to a boil salted water in a pot over high heat.

2. Add in the remaining vinegar and a pinch of salt. Drop the eggs, one at a time, and poach for 2-3 minutes until the whites are set and yolks are cooked. Remove with a perforated spoon to a paper towel to drain. Spread the avocado mash on the bread toasts and top with poached eggs to serve.

Nutrition:

- Info Per Serving: Calories: 296;Fat: 24.3g;Protein: 8g;Carbs: 14g.

Apple-tahini Toast

Servings:1
Cooking Time: 0 Minutes
Ingredients:

- 2 slices whole-wheat bread, toasted
- 2 tablespoons tahini
- 1 small apple of your choice, cored and thinly sliced
- 1 teaspoon honey

Directions:
1. Spread the tahini on the toasted bread.
2. Place the apple slices on the bread and drizzle with the honey. Serve immediately.

Nutrition:

- Info Per Serving: Calories: 458;Fat: 17.8g;Protein: 11.0g;Carbs: 63.5g.

Maple-vanilla Yogurt With Walnuts

Servings:4
Cooking Time:10 Minutes
Ingredients:
- 2 cups Greek yogurt
- ¾ cup maple syrup
- 1 cup walnuts, chopped
- 1 tsp vanilla extract
- 2 tsp cinnamon powder

Directions:
1. Combine yogurt, walnuts, vanilla, maple syrup, and cinnamon powder in a bowl. Let sit in the fridge for 10 minutes.

Nutrition:
- Info Per Serving: Calories: 400;Fat: 25g;Protein: 11g;Carbs: 40g.

Easy Alfalfa Sprout And Nut Rolls

Servings:16
Cooking Time: 0 Minutes
Ingredients:
- 1 cup alfalfa sprouts
- 2 tablespoons Brazil nuts
- ½ cup chopped fresh cilantro
- 2 tablespoons flaked coconut
- 1 garlic clove, minced
- 2 tablespoons ground flaxseeds
- Zest and juice of 1 lemon
- Pinch cayenne pepper
- Sea salt and freshly ground black pepper, to taste
- 1 tablespoon melted coconut oil
- 2 tablespoons water
- 2 whole-grain wraps

Directions:
1. Combine all ingredients, except for the wraps, in a food processor, then pulse to combine well until smooth.
2. Unfold the wraps on a clean work surface, then spread the mixture over the wraps. Roll the wraps up and refrigerate for 30 minutes until set.
3. Remove the rolls from the refrigerator and slice into 16 bite-sized pieces, if desired, and serve.

Nutrition:
- Info Per Serving: Calories: 67;Fat: 7.1g;Protein: 2.2g;Carbs: 2.9g.

Cream Peach Smoothie

Servings:1
Cooking Time:5 Minutes

Ingredients:
- 1 large peach, sliced
- 6 oz peach Greek yogurt
- 2 tbsp almond milk
- 2 ice cubes

Directions:
1. Blend the peach, yogurt, almond milk, and ice cubes in your food processor until thick and creamy. Serve and enjoy!

Nutrition:
- Info Per Serving: Calories: 228;Fat: 3g;Protein 11g;Carbs: 41.6g.

Cheesy Broccoli And Mushroom Egg Casserole

Servings:4
Cooking Time: 40 Minutes
Ingredients:
- 2 tablespoons extra-virgin olive oil
- ½ sweet onion, chopped
- 1 teaspoon minced garlic
- 1 cup sliced button mushrooms
- 1 cup chopped broccoli
- 8 large eggs
- ¼ cup unsweetened almond milk
- 1 tablespoon chopped fresh basil
- 1 cup shredded Cheddar cheese
- Sea salt and freshly ground black pepper, to taste

Directions:
1. Preheat the oven to 375°F.
2. Heat the olive oil in a large ovenproof skillet over medium-high heat.
3. Add the onion, garlic, and mushrooms to the skillet and sauté for about 5 minutes, stirring occasionally.
4. Stir in the broccoli and sauté for 5 minutes until the vegetables start to soften.
5. Meanwhile, beat the eggs with the almond milk and basil in a small bowl until well mixed.
6. Remove the skillet from the heat and pour the egg mixture over the top. Scatter the Cheddar cheese over.
7. Bake uncovered in the preheated oven for about 3 minutes, or until the top of the casserole is golden brown and a fork inserted in the center comes out clean.
8. Remove from the oven and sprinkle with the sea salt and pepper. Serve hot.

Nutrition:
- Info Per Serving: Calories: 326;Fat: 27.2g;Protein 14.1g;Carbs: 6.7g.

Pumpkin-yogurt Parfaits

Servings:4
Cooking Time:5 Min + Chilling Time
Ingredients:

- 1 can pumpkin puree
- 4 tsp honey
- 1 tsp pumpkin pie spice
- ¼ tsp ground cinnamon
- 2 cups Greek yogurt
- 1 cup honey granola
- 2 tbsp pomegranate seeds

Directions:

1. Mix the pumpkin puree, honey, pumpkin pie spice, and cinnamon in a large bowl. Layer the pumpkin mix, yogurt, and granola in small glasses. Repeat the layers. Top with pomegranate seeds. Chill for at least 3 hours before serving.

Nutrition:

- Info Per Serving: Calories: 264;Fat: 9.2g;Protein: 15g;Carbs: 35g.

Vegetable Mains And Meatless Recipes

Cauliflower Rice Risotto With Mushrooms

Servings:4
Cooking Time: 10 Minutes
Ingredients:

- 1 teaspoon extra-virgin olive oil
- ½ cup chopped portobello mushrooms
- 4 cups cauliflower rice
- ½ cup half-and-half
- ¼ cup low-sodium vegetable broth
- 1 cup shredded Parmesan cheese

Directions:

1. In a medium skillet, heat the olive oil over medium-low heat until shimmering.
2. Add the mushrooms and stir-fry for 3 minutes.
3. Stir in the cauliflower rice, half-and-half, and vegetable broth. Cover and bring to a boil over high heat for 5 minutes, stirring occasionally.
4. Add the Parmesan cheese and stir to combine. Continue cooking for an additional 3 minutes until the cheese is melted.
5. Divide the mixture into four bowls and serve warm.

Nutrition:

- Info Per Serving: Calories: 167;Fat: 10.7g;Protein: 12.1g;Carbs: 8.1g.

Buttery Garlic Green Beans

Servings:6
Cooking Time:25 Minutes
Ingredients:

- 2 tbsp butter
- 1 lb green beans, trimmed
- 4 cups water
- 6 garlic cloves, minced
- 1 shallot, chopped
- Celery salt to taste
- ½ tsp red pepper flakes

Directions:

1. Pour 4 cups of water in a pot over high heat and bring to a boil. Cut the green beans in half crosswise. Reduce the heat and add in the green beans. Simmer for 6-8 minutes until crisp-tender but still vibrant green. Drain beans and set aside.
2. Melt the butter in a pan over medium heat and sauté garlic and shallot for 3 minutes until the garlic is slightly browned and fragrant. Stir in the beans and season with celery salt. Cook for 2–3 minutes. Serve topped with red pepper flakes.

Nutrition:

- Info Per Serving: Calories: 65;Fat: 4g;Protein: 2g;Carbs: 7g.

Veggie Rice Bowls With Pesto Sauce

Servings:2
Cooking Time: 1 Minute
Ingredients:
- 2 cups water
- 1 cup arborio rice, rinsed
- Salt and ground black pepper, to taste
- 2 eggs
- 1 cup broccoli florets
- ½ pound Brussels sprouts
- 1 carrot, peeled and chopped
- 1 small beet, peeled and cubed
- ¼ cup pesto sauce
- Lemon wedges, for serving

Directions:
1. Combine the water, rice, salt, and pepper in the Instant Pot. Insert a trivet over rice and place a steamer basket on top. Add the eggs, broccoli, Brussels sprouts, carrots, beet cubes, salt, and pepper to the steamer basket.
2. Lock the lid. Select the Manual mode and set the cooking time for 1 minute at High Pressure.
3. When the timer beeps, perform a natural pressure release for 10 minutes, then release any remaining pressure. Carefully open the lid.
4. Remove the steamer basket and trivet from the pot and transfer the eggs to a bowl of ice water. Peel and halve the eggs. Use a fork to fluff the rice.
5. Divide the rice, broccoli, Brussels sprouts, carrot, beet cubes, and eggs into two bowls. Top with a dollop of pesto sauce and serve with the lemon wedges.

Nutrition:
- Info Per Serving: Calories: 590;Fat: 34.1g;Protein: 21.9g;Carbs: 50.0g.

Tomatoes Filled With Tabbouleh

Servings:4
Cooking Time:25 Minutes
Ingredients:
- 3 tbsp olive oil, divided
- 8 medium tomatoes
- ½ cup water
- ½ cup bulgur wheat
- 1 ½ cups minced parsley
- ⅓ cup minced fresh mint
- 2 scallions, chopped
- 1 tsp sumac
- Salt and black pepper to taste
- 1 lemon, zested

Directions:
1. Place the bulgur wheat and 2 cups of salted water in a pot and bring to a boil. Lower the heat and simmer for 10 minutes or until tender. Remove the pot from the heat and cover with a lid. Let it sit for 15 minutes.
2. Preheat the oven to 400 F. Slice off the top of each tomato and scoop out the pulp and seeds using a spoon into a sieve set over a bowl. Drain and discard any excess liquid; chop the remaining pulp and place it in a large mixing bowl. Add in parsley, mint, scallions, sumac, lemon zest, lemon juice, bulgur, pepper, and salt, and mix well.
3. Spoon the filling into the tomatoes and place the lids on top. Drizzle with olive oil and bake for 15-20 minutes until the tomatoes are tender. Serve and enjoy

Nutrition:
- Info Per Serving: Calories: 160;Fat: 7g;Protein: 5g;Carbs: 22g.

Stir-fry Baby Bok Choy

Servings:6
Cooking Time: 10 To 13 Minutes
Ingredients:
- 2 tablespoons coconut oil
- 1 large onion, finely diced
- 2 teaspoons ground cumin
- 1-inch piece fresh ginger, grated
- 1 teaspoon ground turmeric
- ½ teaspoon salt
- 12 baby bok choy heads, ends trimmed and sliced lengthwise
- Water, as needed
- 3 cups cooked brown rice

Directions:
1. Heat the coconut oil in a large pan over medium heat.
2. Sauté the onion for 5 minutes, stirring occasionally, or until the onion is translucent.
3. Fold in the cumin, ginger, turmeric, and salt and stir to coat well.
4. Add the bok choy and cook for 5 to 8 minutes, stirring occasionally, or until the bok choy is tender but crisp. You can add 1 tablespoon of water at a time, if the skillet gets dry until you finish sautéing.
5. Transfer the bok choy to a plate and serve over the cooked brown rice.

Nutrition:
- Info Per Serving: Calories: 443;Fat: 8.8g;Protein: 30.3g;Carbs: 75.7g.

Brussels Sprouts Linguine

Servings:4
Cooking Time: 25 Minutes
Ingredients:

- 8 ounces whole-wheat linguine
- ⅓ cup plus 2 tablespoons extra-virgin olive oil, divided
- 1 medium sweet onion, diced
- 2 to 3 garlic cloves, smashed
- 8 ounces Brussels sprouts, chopped
- ½ cup chicken stock
- ⅓ cup dry white wine
- ½ cup shredded Parmesan cheese
- 1 lemon, quartered

Directions:

1. Bring a large pot of water to a boil and cook the pasta for about 5 minutes, or until al dente. Drain the pasta and reserve 1 cup of the pasta water. Mix the cooked pasta with 2 tablespoons of the olive oil. Set aside.

2. In a large skillet, heat the remaining ⅓ cup of the olive oil over medium heat. Add the onion to the skillet and sauté for about 4 minutes, or until tender. Add the smashed garlic cloves and sauté for 1 minute, or until fragrant.

3. Stir in the Brussels sprouts and cook covered for 10 minutes. Pour in the chicken stock to prevent burning. Once the Brussels sprouts have wilted and are fork-tender, add white wine and cook for about 5 minutes, or until reduced.

4. Add the pasta to the skillet and add the pasta water as needed.

5. Top with the Parmesan cheese and squeeze the lemon over the dish right before eating.

Nutrition:

Info Per Serving: Calories: 502;Fat: 31.0g;Protein: 15.0g;Carbs: 50.0g.

Parsley & Olive Zucchini Bake

Servings:6
Cooking Time:1 Hour 40 Minutes
Ingredients:

- 3 tbsp olive oil
- 1 can tomatoes, diced
- 2 lb zucchinis, sliced
- 1 onion, chopped
- Salt and black pepper to taste
- 3 garlic cloves, minced

- ¼ tsp dried oregano
- ¼ tsp red pepper flakes
- 10 Kalamata olives, chopped
- 2 tbsp fresh parsley, chopped

Directions:

1. Preheat oven to 325 F. Warm the olive oil in a saucepan over medium heat. Sauté zucchini for about 3 minutes per side; transfer to a bowl. Stir-fry the onion and salt in the same saucepan for 3-5 minutes, stirring occasionally until onion soft and lightly golden. Stir in garlic, oregano, and pepper flakes and cook until fragrant, about 30 seconds.

2. Add in olives, tomatoes, salt, and pepper, bring to a simmer, and cook for about 10 minutes, stirring occasionally. Return the zucchini, cover, and transfer the pot to the oven. Bake for 10-15 minutes. Sprinkle with parsley and serve.

Nutrition:

- Info Per Serving: Calories: 164;Fat: 6g;Protein: 1.5g;Carbs: 7.7g.

Vegetable And Red Lentil Stew

Servings:6
Cooking Time: 35 Minutes
Ingredients:

- 1 tablespoon extra-virgin olive oil
- 2 onions, peeled and finely diced
- 6½ cups water
- 2 zucchinis, finely diced
- 4 celery stalks, finely diced
- 3 cups red lentils
- 1 teaspoon dried oregano
- 1 teaspoon salt, plus more as needed

Directions:

1. Heat the olive oil in a large pot over medium heat.

2. Add the onions and sauté for about 5 minutes, stirring constantly, or until the onions are softened.

3. Stir in the water, zucchini, celery, lentils, oregano, and salt and bring the mixture to a boil.

4. Reduce the heat to low and let simmer covered for 30 minutes, stirring occasionally, or until the lentils are tender.

5. Taste and adjust the seasoning as needed.

Nutrition:

- Info Per Serving: Calories: 387;Fat: 4.4g;Protein: 24.0g;Carbs: 63.7g.

Garlic-butter Asparagus With Parmesan

Servings:2
Cooking Time: 8 Minutes
Ingredients:
- 1 cup water
- 1 pound asparagus, trimmed
- 2 cloves garlic, chopped
- 3 tablespoons almond butter
- Salt and ground black pepper, to taste
- 3 tablespoons grated Parmesan cheese

Directions:
1. Pour the water into the Instant Pot and insert a trivet.
2. Put the asparagus on a tin foil add the butter and garlic. Season to taste with salt and pepper.
3. Fold over the foil and seal the asparagus inside so the foil doesn't come open. Arrange the asparagus on the trivet.
4. Secure the lid. Select the Manual mode and set the cooking time for 8 minutes at High Pressure.
5. Once cooking is complete, do a quick pressure release. Carefully open the lid.
6. Unwrap the foil packet and serve sprinkled with the Parmesan cheese.

Nutrition:
- Info Per Serving: Calories: 243;Fat: 15.7g;Protein: 12.3g;Carbs: 15.3g.

Sweet Pepper Stew

Servings:2
Cooking Time: 50 Minutes
Ingredients:
- 2 tablespoons olive oil
- 2 sweet peppers, diced
- ½ large onion, minced
- 1 garlic clove, minced
- 1 tablespoon gluten-free Worcestershire sauce
- 1 teaspoon oregano
- 1 cup low-sodium tomato juice
- 1 cup low-sodium vegetable stock
- ¼ cup brown rice
- ¼ cup brown lentils
- Salt, to taste

Directions:
1. In a Dutch oven, heat the olive oil over medium-high heat.
2. Sauté the sweet peppers and onion for 10 minutes stirring occasionally, or until the onion begins to turn golden and the peppers are wilted.
3. Stir in the garlic, Worcestershire sauce, and oregano and cook for 30 seconds more. Add the tomato juice, vegetable stock, rice, and lentils to the Dutch oven and stir to mix well.
4. Bring the mixture to a boil and then reduce the heat to medium-low. Let it simmer covered for about 45 minutes, or until the rice is cooked through and the lentils are tender.
5. Sprinkle with salt and serve warm.

Nutrition:
- Info Per Serving: Calories: 378;Fat: 15.6g;Protein: 11.4g;Carbs: 52.8g.

Roasted Vegetable Medley

Servings:2
Cooking Time:65 Minutes
Ingredients:
- 1 head garlic, cloves split apart, unpeeled
- 3 tbsp olive oil
- 2 carrots, cut into strips
- ¼ lb asparagus, chopped
- ½ lb Brussels sprouts, halved
- 2 cups broccoli florets
- 1 cup cherry tomatoes
- ½ fresh lemon, sliced
- Salt and black pepper to taste

Directions:
1. Preheat oven to 375 F. Drizzle the garlic cloves with some olive oil and lightly wrap them in a small piece of foil. Place the packet in the oven and roast for 30 minutes. Place all the vegetables and the lemon slices into a large mixing bowl. Drizzle with the remaining olive oil and season with salt and pepper. Increase the oven to 400 F. Pour the vegetables on a sheet pan in a single layer, leaving the packet of garlic cloves on the pan. Roast for 20 minutes, shaking occasionally until tender. Remove the pan from the oven. Let the garlic cloves sit until cool enough to handle, then remove the skins. Top the vegetables with roasted garlic and serve.

Nutrition:
- Info Per Serving: Calories: 256;Fat: 15g;Protein: 7g;Carbs: 31g.

Moroccan Tagine With Vegetables

Servings:2

Cooking Time: 40 Minutes

Ingredients:

- 2 tablespoons olive oil
- ½ onion, diced
- 1 garlic clove, minced
- 2 cups cauliflower florets
- 1 medium carrot, cut into 1-inch pieces
- 1 cup diced eggplant
- 1 can whole tomatoes with their juices
- 1 can chickpeas, drained and rinsed
- 2 small red potatoes, cut into 1-inch pieces
- 1 cup water
- 1 teaspoon pure maple syrup
- ½ teaspoon cinnamon
- ½ teaspoon turmeric
- 1 teaspoon cumin
- ½ teaspoon salt
- 1 to 2 teaspoons harissa paste

Directions:

1. In a Dutch oven, heat the olive oil over medium-high heat. Sauté the onion for 5 minutes, stirring occasionally, or until the onion is translucent.

2. Stir in the garlic, cauliflower florets, carrot, eggplant, tomatoes, and potatoes. Using a wooden spoon or spatula to break up the tomatoes into smaller pieces.

3. Add the chickpeas, water, maple syrup, cinnamon, turmeric, cumin, and salt and stir to incorporate. Bring the mixture to a boil.

4. Once it starts to boil, reduce the heat to medium-low. Stir in the harissa paste, cover, allow to simmer for about 40 minutes, or until the vegetables are softened. Taste and adjust seasoning as needed.

5. Let the mixture cool for 5 minutes before serving.

Nutrition:

- Info Per Serving: Calories: 293;Fat: 9.9g;Protein: 11.2g;Carbs: 45.5g.

Celery And Mustard Greens

Servings:4

Cooking Time: 15 Minutes

Ingredients:

- ½ cup low-sodium vegetable broth
- 1 celery stalk, roughly chopped
- ½ sweet onion, chopped
- ½ large red bell pepper, thinly sliced
- 2 garlic cloves, minced
- 1 bunch mustard greens, roughly chopped

Directions:

1. Pour the vegetable broth into a large cast iron pan and bring it to a simmer over medium heat.

2. Stir in the celery, onion, bell pepper, and garlic. Cook uncovered for about 3 to 5 minutes, or until the onion is softened.

3. Add the mustard greens to the pan and stir well. Cover, reduce the heat to low, and cook for an additional 10 minutes, or until the liquid is evaporated and the greens are wilted.

4. Remove from the heat and serve warm.

Nutrition:

- Info Per Serving: Calories: 39;Fat: 0g;Protein: 3.1g;Carbs: 6.8g.

Lentil And Tomato Collard Wraps

Servings:4

Cooking Time: 0 Minutes

Ingredients:

- 2 cups cooked lentils
- 5 Roma tomatoes, diced
- ½ cup crumbled feta cheese
- 10 large fresh basil leaves, thinly sliced
- ¼ cup extra-virgin olive oil
- 1 tablespoon balsamic vinegar
- 2 garlic cloves, minced
- ½ teaspoon raw honey
- ½ teaspoon salt
- ¼ teaspoon freshly ground black pepper
- 4 large collard leaves, stems removed

Directions:

1. Combine the lentils, tomatoes, cheese, basil leaves, olive oil, vinegar, garlic, honey, salt, and black pepper in a large bowl and stir until well blended.

2. Lay the collard leaves on a flat work surface. Spoon the equal-sized amounts of the lentil mixture onto the edges of the leaves. Roll them up and slice in half to serve.

Nutrition:

- Info Per Serving: Calories: 318;Fat: 17.6g;Protein: 13.2g;Carbs: 27.5g.

Butternut Noodles With Mushrooms

Servings:4
Cooking Time: 12 Minutes
Ingredients:

- ¼ cup extra-virgin olive oil
- 1 pound cremini mushrooms, sliced
- ½ red onion, finely chopped
- 1 teaspoon dried thyme
- ½ teaspoon sea salt
- 3 garlic cloves, minced
- ½ cup dry white wine
- Pinch of red pepper flakes
- 4 cups butternut noodles
- 4 ounces grated Parmesan cheese

Directions:

1. In a large skillet over medium-high heat, heat the olive oil until shimmering. Add the mushrooms, onion, thyme, and salt to the skillet. Cook for about 6 minutes, stirring occasionally, or until the mushrooms start to brown. Add the garlic and sauté for 30 seconds. Stir in the white wine and red pepper flakes.
2. Fold in the noodles. Cook for about 5 minutes, stirring occasionally, or until the noodles are tender.
3. Serve topped with the grated Parmesan.

Nutrition:

- Info Per Serving: Calories: 244;Fat: 14.0g;Protein: 4.0g;Carbs: 22.0g.

Zucchini Crisp

Servings:2
Cooking Time: 20 Minutes
Ingredients:

- 4 zucchinis, sliced into ½-inch rounds
- ½ cup unsweetened almond milk
- 1 teaspoon fresh lemon juice
- 1 teaspoon arrowroot powder
- ½ teaspoon salt, divided
- ½ cup whole wheat bread crumbs
- ¼ cup nutritional yeast
- ¼ cup hemp seeds
- ½ teaspoon garlic powder
- ¼ teaspoon crushed red pepper
- ¼ teaspoon black pepper

Directions:

1. Preheat the oven to 375°F. Line two baking sheets with parchment paper and set aside.

2. Put the zucchini in a medium bowl with the almond milk, lemon juice, arrowroot powder, and ¼ teaspoon of salt. Stir to mix well.
3. In a large bowl with a lid, thoroughly combine the bread crumbs, nutritional yeast, hemp seeds, garlic powder, crushed red pepper and black pepper. Add the zucchini in batches and shake until the slices are evenly coated.
4. Arrange the zucchini on the prepared baking sheet in a single layer.
5. Bake in the preheated oven for about 20 minutes or until the zucchini slices are golden brown.
6. Season with the remaining ¼ teaspoon of salt before serving.

Nutrition:

- Info Per Serving: Calories: 255;Fat: 11.3g;Protein 8.6g;Carbs: 31.9g.

Sweet Mustard Cabbage Hash

Servings:4
Cooking Time:30 Minutes
Ingredients:

- 1 head Savoy cabbage, shredded
- 3 tbsp olive oil
- 1 onion, finely chopped
- 2 garlic cloves, minced
- ½ tsp fennel seeds
- ¼ cup red wine vinegar
- 1 tbsp mustard powder
- 1 tbsp honey
- Salt and black pepper to taste

Directions:

1. Warm olive oil in a pan over medium heat and sauté onion, fennel seeds, cabbage, salt, and pepper for 8-9 minutes.
2. In a bowl, mix vinegar, mustard, and honey; set aside. Sauté garlic in the pan for 30 seconds. Pour in vinegar mixture and cook for 10-15 minutes until the liquid reduces by half.

Nutrition:

- Info Per Serving: Calories: 181;Fat: 12g;Protein 3.4g;Carbs: 19g.

Baked Honey Acorn Squash

Servings:4
Cooking Time:35 Minutes
Ingredients:

- 1 acorn squash, cut into wedges
- 2 tbsp olive oil
- 2 tbsp honey
- 2 tbsp rosemary, chopped
- 2 tbsp walnuts, chopped

Directions:

Preheat oven to 400 F. In a bowl, mix honey, rosemary, and olive oil. Lay the squash wedges on a baking sheet and drizzle with the honey mixture. Bake for 30 minutes until squash is tender and slightly caramelized, turning each slice over halfway through. Serve cooled sprinkled with walnuts.

Nutrition:

- Info Per Serving: Calories: 136;Fat: 6g;Protein: .9g;Carbs: 20g.

Mushroom & Cauliflower Roast

Servings:4
Cooking Time:35 Minutes
Ingredients:

- 2 tbsp olive oil
- 4 cups cauliflower florets
- 1 celery stalk, chopped
- 1 cup mushrooms, sliced
- 10 cherry tomatoes, halved
- 1 yellow onion, chopped
- 2 garlic cloves, minced
- 2 tbsp dill, chopped
- Salt and black pepper to taste

Directions:

Preheat the oven to 340 F. Line a baking sheet with parchment paper. Place in cauliflower florets, olive oil, mushrooms, celery, tomatoes, onion, garlic, salt, and pepper and mix to combine. Bake for 25 minutes. Serve topped with dill.

Nutrition:

- Info Per Serving: Calories: 380;Fat: 15g;Protein: 2g;Carbs: 17g.

Balsamic Cherry Tomatoes

Servings:4
Cooking Time:10 Minutes
Ingredients:

- 2 tbsp olive oil
- 2 lb cherry tomatoes, halved
- 2 tbsp balsamic glaze
- Salt and black pepper to taste
- 1 garlic clove, minced
- 2 tbsp fresh basil, torn

Directions:

1. Warm the olive oil in a skillet over medium heat. Add the cherry tomatoes and cook for 1-2 minutes, stirring occasionally. Stir in garlic, salt, and pepper and cook until fragrant, about 30 seconds. Drizzle with balsamic glaze and decorate with basil. Serve and enjoy!

Nutrition:

- Info Per Serving: Calories: 45;Fat: 2.5g;Protein: 1.1g;Carbs: 5.6g.

Roasted Celery Root With Yogurt Sauce

Servings:6
Cooking Time:50 Minutes
Ingredients:

- 3 tbsp olive oil
- 3 celery roots, sliced
- Salt and black pepper to taste
- ¼ cup plain yogurt
- ¼ tsp grated lemon zest
- 1 tsp lemon juice
- 1 tsp sesame seeds, toasted
- 1 tsp coriander seeds, crushed
- ¼ tsp dried thyme
- ¼ tsp chili powder
- ¼ cup fresh cilantro, chopped

Directions:

1. Preheat oven to 425 F. Place the celery slices on a baking sheet. Sprinkle them with olive oil, salt, and pepper. Roast for 25-30 minutes. Flip each piece and continue to roast for 10-15 minutes until celery root is very tender and sides touching sheet are browned. Transfer celery to a serving platter.

2. Whisk yogurt, lemon zest and juice, and salt together in a bowl. In a separate bowl, combine sesame seeds, coriander seeds, thyme, chili powder, and salt. Drizzle celery root with yogurt sauce and sprinkle with seed mixture and cilantro.

Nutrition:

- Info Per Serving: Calories: 75;Fat: 7.5g;Protein: 0.7g;Carbs: 1.8g.

Fried Eggplant Rolls

Servings:4
Cooking Time: 10 Minutes
Ingredients:
- 2 large eggplants, trimmed and cut lengthwise into ¼-inch-thick slices
- 1 teaspoon salt
- 1 cup shredded ricotta cheese
- 4 ounces goat cheese, shredded
- ¼ cup finely chopped fresh basil
- ½ teaspoon freshly ground black pepper
- Olive oil spray

Directions:
1. Add the eggplant slices to a colander and season with salt. Set aside for 15 to 20 minutes.
2. Mix together the ricotta and goat cheese, basil, and black pepper in a large bowl and stir to combine. Set aside.
3. Dry the eggplant slices with paper towels and lightly mist them with olive oil spray.
4. Heat a large skillet over medium heat and lightly spray it with olive oil spray.
5. Arrange the eggplant slices in the skillet and fry each side for 3 minutes until golden brown.
6. Remove from the heat to a paper towel-lined plate and rest for 5 minutes.
7. Make the eggplant rolls: Lay the eggplant slices on a flat work surface and top each slice with a tablespoon of the prepared cheese mixture. Roll them up and serve immediately.

Nutrition:
- Info Per Serving: Calories: 254;Fat: 14.9g;Protein: 15.3g;Carbs: 18.6g.

Balsamic Grilled Vegetables

Servings:4
Cooking Time:20 Minutes
Ingredients:
- ¼ cup olive oil
- 4 carrots, cut in half
- 2 onions, quartered
- 1 zucchini, cut into rounds
- 1 eggplant, cut into rounds
- 1 red bell pepper, chopped
- Salt and black pepper to taste
- Balsamic vinegar to taste

Directions:
1. Heat your grill to medium-high. Brush the vegetables lightly with olive oil, and season with salt and pepper. Grill the vegetables for 3–4 minutes per side. Transfer to a serving dish and drizzle with balsamic vinegar. Serve and enjoy!

Nutrition:

- Info Per Serving: Calories: 184;Fat: 14g;Protein 2.1g;Carbs: 14g.

Roasted Veggies And Brown Rice Bowl

Servings:4
Cooking Time: 20 Minutes
Ingredients:
- 2 cups cauliflower florets
- 2 cups broccoli florets
- 1 can chickpeas, drained and rinsed
- 1 cup carrot slices
- 2 to 3 tablespoons extra-virgin olive oil, divided
- Salt and freshly ground black pepper, to taste
- Nonstick cooking spray
- 2 cups cooked brown rice
- 2 to 3 tablespoons sesame seeds, for garnish
- Dressing:
- 3 to 4 tablespoons tahini
- 2 tablespoons honey
- 1 lemon, juiced
- 1 garlic clove, minced
- Salt and freshly ground black pepper, to taste

Directions:
1. Preheat the oven to 400°F. Spritz two baking sheets with nonstick cooking spray.
2. Spread the cauliflower and broccoli on the first baking sheet and the second with the chickpeas and carrot slices.
3. Drizzle each sheet with half of the olive oil and sprinkle with salt and pepper. Toss to coat well.
4. Roast the chickpeas and carrot slices in the preheated oven for 10 minutes, leaving the carrot tender but crisp, and the cauliflower and broccoli for 20 minutes until fork-tender. Stir them once halfway through the cooking time.
5. Meanwhile, make the dressing: Whisk together the tahini, honey, lemon juice, garlic, salt, and pepper in a small bowl.
6. Divide the cooked brown rice among four bowls. Top each bowl evenly with roasted vegetables and dressing. Sprinkle the sesame seeds on top for garnish before serving.

Nutrition:
- Info Per Serving: Calories: 453;Fat: 17.8g;Protein 12.1g;Carbs: 61.8g.

Braised Cauliflower With White Wine

Servings:4
Cooking Time: 12 To 16 Minutes
Ingredients:
- 3 tablespoons plus 1 teaspoon extra-virgin olive oil, divided
- 3 garlic cloves, minced
- ⅛ teaspoon red pepper flakes
- 1 head cauliflower, cored and cut into 1½-inch florets
- ¼ teaspoon salt, plus more for seasoning
- Black pepper, to taste
- ⅓ cup vegetable broth
- ⅓ cup dry white wine
- 2 tablespoons minced fresh parsley

Directions:
1. Combine 1 teaspoon of the oil, garlic and pepper flakes in small bowl.
2. Heat the remaining 3 tablespoons of the oil in a skillet over medium-high heat until shimmering. Add the cauliflower and ¼ teaspoon of the salt and cook for 7 to 9 minutes, stirring occasionally, or until florets are golden brown.
3. Push the cauliflower to sides of the skillet. Add the garlic mixture to the center of the skillet. Cook for about 30 seconds, or until fragrant. Stir the garlic mixture into the cauliflower.
4. Pour in the broth and wine and bring to simmer. Reduce the heat to medium-low. Cover and cook for 4 to 6 minutes, or until the cauliflower is crisp-tender. Off heat, stir in the parsley and season with salt and pepper.
5. Serve immediately.

Nutrition:
- Info Per Serving: Calories: 143;Fat: 11.7g;Protein: 3.1g;Carbs: 8.7g.

Garlicky Broccoli Rabe

Servings:4
Cooking Time: 5 To 6 Minutes
Ingredients:
- 14 ounces broccoli rabe, trimmed and cut into 1-inch pieces
- 2 teaspoons salt, plus more for seasoning
- Black pepper, to taste
- 2 tablespoons extra-virgin olive oil
- 3 garlic cloves, minced
- ¼ teaspoon red pepper flakes

Directions:
1. Bring 3 quarts water to a boil in a large saucepan. Add the broccoli rabe and 2 teaspoons of the salt to the boiling water and cook for 2 to 3 minutes, or until wilted and tender.
2. Drain the broccoli rabe. Transfer to ice water and let sit until chilled. Drain again and pat dry.
3. In a skillet over medium heat, heat the oil and add the garlic and red pepper flakes. Sauté for about 2 minutes, or until the garlic begins to sizzle.
4. Increase the heat to medium-high. Stir in the broccoli rabe and cook for about 1 minute, or until heated through, stirring constantly. Season with salt and pepper.
5. Serve immediately.

Nutrition:
- Info Per Serving: Calories: 87;Fat: 7.3g;Protein: 3.4g;Carbs: 4.0g.

Parmesan Stuffed Zucchini Boats

Servings:4
Cooking Time: 15 Minutes
Ingredients:
- 1 cup canned low-sodium chickpeas, drained and rinsed
- 1 cup no-sugar-added spaghetti sauce
- 2 zucchinis
- ¼ cup shredded Parmesan cheese

Directions:
1. Preheat the oven to 425°F.
2. In a medium bowl, stir together the chickpeas and spaghetti sauce.
3. Cut the zucchini in half lengthwise and scrape a spoon gently down the length of each half to remove the seeds.
4. Fill each zucchini half with the chickpea sauce and top with one-quarter of the Parmesan cheese.
5. Place the zucchini halves on a baking sheet and roast in the oven for 15 minutes.
6. Transfer to a plate. Let rest for 5 minutes before serving.

Nutrition:
- Info Per Serving: Calories: 139;Fat: 4.0g;Protein: 8.0g;Carbs: 20.0g.

Simple Zoodles

Servings:2
Cooking Time: 5 Minutes
Ingredients:
- 2 tablespoons avocado oil
- 2 medium zucchinis, spiralized
- ¼ teaspoon salt
- Freshly ground black pepper, to taste

Directions:
1. Heat the avocado oil in a large skillet over medium heat until it shimmers.
2. Add the zucchini noodles, salt, and black pepper to the skillet and toss to coat. Cook for 1 to 2 minutes, stirring constantly, until tender.
3. Serve warm.

Nutrition:
- Info Per Serving: Calories: 128;Fat: 14.0g;Protein: 0.3g;Carbs: 0.3g.

Baked Beet & Leek With Dilly Yogurt

Servings:4

Cooking Time:40 Minutes
Ingredients:
- 5 tbsp olive oil
- ½ lb leeks, thickly sliced
- 1 lb red beets, sliced
- 1 cup yogurt
- 2 garlic cloves, finely minced
- ¼ tsp cumin, ground
- ¼ tsp dried parsley
- ¼ cup parsley, chopped
- 1 tsp dill
- Salt and black pepper to taste

Directions:
1. Preheat the oven to 390 F. Arrange the beets and leeks on a greased roasting dish. Sprinkle with some olive oil, cumin, dried parsley, black pepper, and salt. Bake in the oven for 25-30 minutes. Transfer to a serving platter. In a bowl, stir in yogurt, dill, garlic, and the remaining olive oil. Whisk to combine. Drizzle the veggies with the yogurt sauce and top with fresh parsley to serve.

Nutrition:
- Info Per Serving: Calories: 281;Fat: 18.7g;Protein 6g;Carbs: 24g.

Beans , Grains, And Pastas Recipes

Oregano Chicken Risotto

Servings:4
Cooking Time:45 Minutes
Ingredients:
- 4 chicken thighs, bone-in and skin-on
- 2 tbsp olive oil
- 1 cup arborio rice
- 2 lemons, juiced
- 1 tsp oregano, dried
- 1 red onion, chopped
- Salt and black pepper to taste
- 2 garlic cloves, minced
- 2 ½ cups chicken stock
- 1 cup green olives, sliced
- 2 tbsp parsley, chopped
- ½ cup Parmesan, grated

Directions:
1. Warm the olive oil in a skillet over medium heat and brown chicken thighs skin-side down for 3-4 minutes, turn, and cook for 3 minutes. Remove to a plate. Place garlic and onion in the same skillet and sauté for 3 minutes. Stir in rice, salt, pepper, oregano, and lemon juice. Add 1 cup of chicken stock, reduce the heat and simmer the rice while stirring until it is absorbed. Add another cup of chicken broth and continue simmering until the stock is absorbed. Pour in the remaining chicken stock and return the chicken cook until the rice is tender. Turn the heat off. Stir in Parmesan cheese and top with olives and parsley. Serve into plates. Enjoy!

Nutrition:
- Info Per Serving: Calories: 450;Fat: 19g;Protein 26g;Carbs: 28g.

Citrusy & Minty Farro

Servings:6
Cooking Time:28 Minutes
Ingredients:

3 tbsp olive oil

1 ½ cups whole farro

Salt and black pepper to taste

1 onion, chopped fine

1 garlic clove, minced

¼ cup chopped fresh cilantro

¼ cup chopped fresh mint

1 tbsp lemon juice

Directions:

Bring 4 quarts of water to boil in a pot. Add farro and season with salt and pepper, bring to a boil and cook until grains are tender with a slight chew, 20-25 minutes. Drain farro, return to the empty pot and cover to keep warm. Heat 2 tbsp of oil in a large skillet over medium heat. Stir-fry onion for 5 minutes. Stir in garlic and cook until fragrant, about 30 seconds. Add the remaining oil and farro and stir-fry for 2 minutes. Remove from heat, stir in cilantro, mint, and lemon juice. Season to taste and serve.

Nutrition:

Info Per Serving: Calories: 322;Fat: 16g;Protein: 4g;Carbs: 24g.

Kale & Feta Couscous

Servings:4
Cooking Time:20 Minutes
Ingredients:

2 tbsp olive oil

1 cup couscous

1 cup kale, chopped

1 tbsp parsley, chopped

3 spring onions, chopped

1 cucumber, chopped

1 tsp allspice

½ lemon, juiced and zested

4 oz feta cheese, crumbled

Directions:

In a bowl, place couscous and cover with hot water. Let sit for 10 minutes and fluff. Warm the olive oil in a skillet over medium heat and sauté onions and allspice for 3 minutes. Stir in the remaining ingredients and cook for 5-6 minutes.

Nutrition:

- Info Per Serving: Calories: 210;Fat: 7g;Protein: 5g;Carbs: 16g.

Freekeh Pilaf With Dates And Pistachios

Servings:4
Cooking Time: 10 Minutes
Ingredients:

- 2 tablespoons extra-virgin olive oil, plus extra for drizzling
- 1 shallot, minced
- 1½ teaspoons grated fresh ginger
- ¼ teaspoon ground coriander
- ¼ teaspoon ground cumin
- Salt and pepper, to taste
- 1¾ cups water
- 1½ cups cracked freekeh, rinsed
- 3 ounces pitted dates, chopped
- ¼ cup shelled pistachios, toasted and coarsely chopped
- 1½ tablespoons lemon juice
- ¼ cup chopped fresh mint

Directions:

1. Set the Instant Pot to Sauté mode and heat the olive oil until shimmering.

2. Add the shallot, ginger, coriander, cumin, salt, and pepper to the pot and cook for about 2 minutes, or until the shallot is softened. Stir in the water and freekeh.

3. Secure the lid. Select the Manual mode and set the cooking time for 4 minutes at High Pressure. Once cooking is complete, do a quick pressure release. Carefully open the lid.

4. Add the dates, pistachios and lemon juice and gently fluff the freekeh with a fork to combine. Season to taste with salt and pepper.

5. Transfer to a serving dish and sprinkle with the mint. Serve drizzled with extra olive oil.

Nutrition:

- Info Per Serving: Calories: 280;Fat: 8.0g;Protein: 8.0g;Carbs: 46.0g.

Israeli Couscous With Asparagus

Servings:6
Cooking Time: 25 Minutes
Ingredients:
- 1½ pounds asparagus spears, ends trimmed and stalks chopped into 1-inch pieces
- 1 garlic clove, minced
- 1 tablespoon extra-virgin olive oil
- ¼ teaspoon freshly ground black pepper
- 1¾ cups water
- 1 box uncooked whole-wheat or regular Israeli couscous
- ¼ teaspoon kosher salt
- 1 cup garlic-and-herb goat cheese, at room temperature

Directions:
1. Preheat the oven to 425°F.
2. In a large bowl, stir together the asparagus, garlic, oil, and pepper. Spread the asparagus on a large, rimmed baking sheet and roast for 10 minutes, stirring a few times. Remove the pan from the oven, and spoon the asparagus into a large serving bowl. Set aside.
3. While the asparagus is roasting, bring the water to a boil in a medium saucepan. Add the couscous and season with salt, stirring well.
4. Reduce the heat to medium-low. Cover and cook for 12 minutes, or until the water is absorbed.
5. Pour the hot couscous into the bowl with the asparagus. Add the goat cheese and mix thoroughly until completely melted.
6. Serve immediately.

Nutrition:
- Info Per Serving: Calories: 103;Fat: 2.0g;Protein: 6.0g;Carbs: 18.0g.

Slow Cooked Turkey And Brown Rice

Servings:6
Cooking Time: 3 Hours 10 Minutes
Ingredients:
- 1 tablespoon extra-virgin olive oil
- 1½ pounds ground turkey
- 2 tablespoons chopped fresh sage, divided
- 2 tablespoons chopped fresh thyme, divided
- 1 teaspoon sea salt
- ½ teaspoon ground black pepper
- 2 cups brown rice
- 1 can stewed tomatoes, with the juice
- ¼ cup pitted and sliced Kalamata olives
- 3 medium zucchini, sliced thinly
- ¼ cup chopped fresh flat-leaf parsley
- 1 medium yellow onion, chopped
- 1 tablespoon plus 1 teaspoon balsamic vinegar
- 2 cups low-sodium chicken stock
- 2 garlic cloves, minced
- ½ cup grated Parmesan cheese, for serving

Directions:
1. Heat the olive oil in a nonstick skillet ov' medium-high heat until shimmering.
2. Add the ground turkey and sprinkle with tablespoon of sage, 1 tablespoon of thyme, salt ar ground black pepper.
3. Sauté for 10 minutes or until the ground turkey lightly browned.
4. Pour them in the slow cooker, then pour in tl remaining ingredients, except for the Parmesan. Stir mix well.
5. Put the lid on and cook on high for 3 hours or un the rice and vegetables are tender.
6. Pour them in a large serving bowl, then sprea with Parmesan cheese before serving.

Nutrition:
- Info Per Serving: Calories: 499;Fat: 16.4g;Protei 32.4g;Carbs: 56.5g.

Paprika Spinach & Chickpea Bow

Servings:4
Cooking Time:20 Minutes
Ingredients:
- 2 tbsp olive oil
- 1 lb canned chickpeas
- 10 oz spinach
- 1 tsp coriander seeds
- 1 red onion, finely chopped
- 2 tomatoes, pureed
- 1 garlic clove, minced
- ½ tbsp rosemary
- ½ tsp smoked paprika
- Salt and white pepper to taste

Directions:
1. Heat the olive oil in a pot over medium heat. Ac in the onion, garlic, coriander seeds, salt, and pepp and cook for 3 minutes until translucent. Stir tomatoes, rosemary, paprika, salt, and white pepp Bring to a boil, then lower the heat, and simmer for minutes. Add in chickpeas and spinach and co covered until the spinach wilts. Serve.

Nutrition:
- Info Per Serving: Calories: 512;Fat: 1.8g;Protei 25g;Carbs: 76g.

Rosemary Barley With Walnuts

Servings:4
Cooking Time:45 Minutes
Ingredients:

- 2 tbsp olive oil
- ½ cup diced onion
- ½ cup diced celery
- 1 carrot, peeled and diced
- 3 cups water
- 1 cup barley
- ½ tsp thyme
- ½ tsp rosemary
- ¼ cup pine nuts
- Salt and black pepper to taste

Directions:

1. Warm the olive oil in a medium saucepan over medium heat. Sauté the onion, celery, and carrot over medium heat until tender. Add the water, barley, and seasonings, and bring to a boil. Reduce the heat and simmer for 23 minutes or until tender. Stir in the pine nuts and season to taste. Serve warm.

Nutrition:

- Info Per Serving: Calories: 276;Fat: 9g;Protein: 7g;Carbs: 41g.

Bean & Egg Noodles With Lemon Sauce

Servings:4
Cooking Time:20 Minutes
Ingredients:

- 3 tbsp olive oil
- 12 oz egg noodles
- 1 can diced tomatoes
- 1 can cannellini beans
- ½ cup heavy cream
- 1 cup vegetable stock
- 2 garlic cloves, minced
- 1 onion, chopped
- 1 cup spinach, chopped
- 1 tsp dill
- 1 tsp thyme
- ½ tsp red pepper, crushed
- 1 tsp lemon juice
- 1 tbsp fresh basil, chopped

Directions:

1. Warm the olive oil in a pot over medium heat. Add in onion and garlic and cook for 3 minutes until softened. Stir in dill, thyme, and red pepper for 1 minute. Add in spinach, vegetable stock, and tomatoes. Bring to a boil, add the egg noodles, cover, and lower the heat. Cook for 5-7 minutes. Put in beans and cook until heated through. Combine the heavy cream, lemon juice, and basil. Serve the dish with creamy lemon sauce on the side.

Nutrition:

- Info Per Serving: Calories: 641;Fat: 19g;Protein: 28g;Carbs: 92g.

Creamy Asparagus & Parmesan Linguine

Servings:2
Cooking Time:30 Minutes
Ingredients:

- 2 tsp olive oil
- 1 bunch of asparagus spears
- 1 yellow onion, thinly sliced
- ¼ cup white wine
- ¼ cup vegetable stock
- 2 cups heavy cream
- ¼ tsp garlic powder
- 8 oz linguine
- ¼ cup Parmesan cheese
- 1 lemon, juiced
- Salt and black pepper to taste
- 2 tbsp chives, chopped

Directions:

1. Bring to a boil salted water in a pot over high heat. Add the linguine and cook according to package directions. Drain and transfer to a bowl. Slice the asparagus into bite-sized pieces. Warm the olive oil in a skillet over medium heat. Add onion and cook 3 minutes until softened. Add asparagus and wine and cook until wine is mostly evaporated, then add the stock. Stir in cream and garlic powder and bring to a boil and simmer until the sauce is slightly thick, 2-3 minutes. Add the linguine and stir until everything is heated through. Remove from the heat and season with lemon juice, salt, and pepper. Top with parmesan cheese and chives and serve.

Nutrition:

- Info Per Serving: Calories: 503;Fat: 55g;Protein: 24g;Carbs: 41g.

Chickpea & Couscous With Apricots

Servings:4
Cooking Time:30 Minutes
Ingredients:

- 2 tbsp olive oil
- 1 red onion, chopped
- 2 garlic cloves, minced
- 14 oz canned chickpeas
- 2 cups veggie stock
- 2 cups couscous, cooked
- ½ cup dried apricots, chopped
- Salt and black pepper to taste

Directions:

1. Warm the olive oil in a skillet over medium heat and cook onion and garlic for 5 minutes. Put in chickpeas, stock, apricots, salt, and pepper and cook for 15 minutes. Ladle couscous into bowls. Top with chickpea mixture.

Nutrition:

- Info Per Serving: Calories: 270;Fat: 12g;Protein: 8g;Carbs: 23g.

Simple Green Rice

Servings:4
Cooking Time:35 Minutes
Ingredients:

- 2 tbsp butter
- 4 spring onions, sliced
- 1 leek, sliced
- 1 medium zucchini, chopped
- 5 oz broccoli florets
- 2 oz curly kale
- ½ cup frozen green peas
- 2 cloves garlic, minced
- 1 thyme sprig, chopped
- 1 rosemary sprig, chopped
- 1 cup white rice
- 2 cups vegetable broth
- 1 large tomato, chopped
- 2 oz Kalamata olives, sliced

Directions:

1. Melt the butter in a saucepan over medium heat. Cook the spring onions, leek, and zucchini for about 4-5 minutes or until tender. Add in the garlic, thyme, and rosemary and continue to sauté for about 1 minute or until aromatic. Add in the rice, broth, and tomato.

Bring to a boil, turn the heat to a gentle simmer, and cook for about 10-12 minutes. Stir in broccoli, kale, and green peas, and continue cooking for 5 minutes. Fluff the rice with a fork and garnish with olives.

Nutrition:

- Info Per Serving: Calories: 403;Fat: 11g;Protein 9g;Carbs: 64g.

Turkish Canned Pinto Bean Salad

Servings:4
Cooking Time: 3 Minutes
Ingredients:

- ¼ cup extra-virgin olive oil, divided
- 3 garlic cloves, lightly crushed and peeled
- 2 cans pinto beans, rinsed
- 2 cups plus 1 tablespoon water
- Salt and pepper, to taste
- ¼ cup tahini
- 3 tablespoons lemon juice
- 1 tablespoon ground dried Aleppo pepper, plu extra for serving
- 8 ounces cherry tomatoes, halved
- ¼ red onion, sliced thinly
- ½ cup fresh parsley leaves
- 2 hard-cooked large eggs, quartered
- 1 tablespoon toasted sesame seeds

Directions:

1. Add 1 tablespoon of the olive oil and garlic to medium saucepan over medium heat. Cook for about minutes, stirring constantly, or until the garlic turn golden but not brown.

2. Add the beans, 2 cups of the water and 1 teaspoo salt and bring to a simmer. Remove from the hea cover and let sit for 20 minutes. Drain the beans an discard the garlic.

3. In a large bowl, whisk together the remaining tablespoons of the oil, tahini, lemon juice, Aleppo, th remaining 1 tablespoon of the water and ¼ teaspoo salt. Stir in the beans, tomatoes, onion and parsle Season with salt and pepper to taste.

4. Transfer to a serving platter and top with the egg Sprinkle with the sesame seeds and extra Alepp before serving.

Nutrition:

- Info Per Serving: Calories: 402;Fat: 18.9g;Protein 16.2g;Carbs: 44.4g.

Chili Pork Rice

Servings:4
Cooking Time:8 Hours 10 Minutes
Ingredients:

- 3 tbsp olive oil
- 2 lb pork loin, sliced
- 1 cup chicken stock
- ½ tbsp chili powder
- 2 tsp thyme, dried
- ½ tbsp garlic powder
- Salt and black pepper to taste
- 2 cups rice, cooked

Directions:

Place pork, chicken stock, oil, chili powder, garlic powder, salt, and pepper in your slow cooker. Cover with the lid and cook for 8 hours on Low. Share pork into plates with a side of rice and garnish with thyme to serve.

Nutrition:

Info Per Serving: Calories: 280;Fat: 15g;Protein: 5g;Carbs: 17g.

Cranberry And Almond Quinoa

Servings:2
Cooking Time: 10 Minutes
Ingredients:

- 2 cups water
- 1 cup quinoa, rinsed
- ¼ cup salted sunflower seeds
- ½ cup slivered almonds
- 1 cup dried cranberries

Directions:

Combine water and quinoa in the Instant Pot.
Secure the lid. Select the Manual mode and set the cooking time for 10 minutes at High Pressure.
Once cooking is complete, do a quick pressure release. Carefully open the lid.
Add sunflower seeds, almonds, and dried cranberries and gently mix until well combined.
Serve hot.

Nutrition:

Info Per Serving: Calories: 445;Fat: 14.8g;Protein: 5.1g;Carbs: 64.1g.

Spicy Rice Bowl With Broccoli & Spinach

Servings:4

Cooking Time:25 Minutes
Ingredients:

- 2 tbsp olive oil
- 12 oz broccoli cuts
- 3 cups fresh baby spinach
- 1 red chili, chopped
- 1 ½ cups cooked brown rice
- 1 onion, chopped
- 1 garlic clove, minced
- 1 orange, juiced and zested
- 1 cup vegetable broth
- Salt and black pepper to taste

Directions:

1. Warm olive oil in a pan over medium heat and sauté onion for 5 minutes, then add in broccoli cuts and cook for 4-5 minutes until tender. Stir-fry garlic and chili for 30 seconds. Pour in orange zest, orange juice, broth, salt, and pepper and bring to a boil. Stir in the rice and spinach and cook for 4 minutes until the liquid is reduced. Serve.

Nutrition:

- Info Per Serving: Calories: 391;Fat: 9.4g;Protein: 9g;Carbs: 67.6g.

Baked Pesto Penne With Broccoli

Servings:4
Cooking Time:40 Minutes
Ingredients:

- 1 lb broccoli florets
- 16 oz penne pasta
- 1 cup vegetable stock
- Salt and black pepper
- 2 tbsp basil pesto
- 2 cups mozzarella, shredded
- 3 tbsp Parmesan cheese, grated
- 2 green onions, chopped

Directions:

1. Bring to a bowl salted water over medium heat and add in the pasta. Cook for 7-9 minutes until al dente. Drain and set aside. Preheat the oven to 380 F. Place pasta, vegetable stock, salt, pepper, basil pesto, broccoli, and green onions in a greased baking pan and combine. Scatter with mozzarella and parmesan cheeses and bake for 30 minutes. Serve.

Nutrition:

- Info Per Serving: Calories: 190;Fat: 4g;Protein: 8g;Carbs: 9g.

Vegetarian Brown Rice Bowl

Servings:4
Cooking Time:25 Minutes
Ingredients:

- ½ lb broccoli rabe, halved lengthways
- 2 tbsp olive oil
- 1 onion, sliced
- 1 red bell pepper, cut into strips
- ½ cup green peas
- 1 carrot, chopped
- 1 celery stalk, chopped
- 1 garlic clove, minced
- ½ cup brown rice
- 2 cups vegetable broth
- Salt and black pepper to taste
- ½ tsp dried thyme
- ¾ tsp paprika
- 2 green onions, chopped

Directions:

1. Warm the olive oil in a skillet over medium heat and sauté onion, garlic, carrot, celery, and bell pepper for 10 minutes. Stir in rice, vegetable broth, salt, pepper, thyme, paprika, and green onions and bring to a simmer. Cook for 15 minutes. Add in broccoli rabe and green peas and cook for 5 minutes.

Nutrition:

- Info Per Serving: Calories: 320;Fat: 5g;Protein: 5g;Carbs: 23g.

Herby Fusilli In Chickpea Sauce

Servings:4
Cooking Time:35 Minutes
Ingredients:

- 1 can chickpeas, drained, liquid reserved
- ¼ cup olive oil
- ½ large shallot, chopped
- 5 garlic cloves, thinly sliced
- 1 cup whole-grain fusilli
- Salt and black pepper to taste
- ¼ cup Parmesan, shaved
- 2 tsp dried parsley
- 1 tsp dried oregano
- A pinch of red pepper flakes

Directions:

1. Heat the oil in a skillet over medium heat and sauté the shallot and garlic for 3-5 minutes until the garlic is golden. Add ¾ of the chickpeas and 2 tbsp of the water from the can; bring to a simmer. Remove from the heat, transfer to a blender, and pulse until smooth. Add the remaining chickpeas and some more of the reserved liquid if it's too thick.

2. Bring a large pot of salted water to a boil and coo pasta until al dente, 7-8 minutes. Reserve ½ cup of t pasta liquid, drain the pasta and return it to the po Add the chickpea sauce to the hot pasta and ke adding ¼ cup of the pasta liquid until your desir consistency is reached. Place the pasta pot ov medium heat and mix occasionally until the sau thickens. Season with salt and pepper. Sprinkle wi freshly grated Parmesan cheese, parsley, oregano, ar red pepper flakes. Serve and enjoy!

Nutrition:

- Info Per Serving: Calories: 322;Fat: 18g;Protei 12g;Carbs: 36g.

Minestrone Chickpeas And Macaroni Casserole

Servings:5
Cooking Time: 7 Hours 20 Minutes
Ingredients:

- 1 can chickpeas, drained and rinsed
- 1 can diced tomatoes, with the juice
- 1 can no-salt-added tomato paste
- 3 medium carrots, sliced
- 3 cloves garlic, minced
- 1 medium yellow onion, chopped
- 1 cup low-sodium vegetable soup
- ½ teaspoon dried rosemary
- 1 teaspoon dried oregano
- 2 teaspoons maple syrup
- ½ teaspoon sea salt
- ¼ teaspoon ground black pepper
- ½ pound fresh green beans, trimmed and cut in bite-size pieces
- 1 cup macaroni pasta
- 2 ounces Parmesan cheese, grated

Directions:

1. Except for the green beans, pasta, and Parmes: cheese, combine all the ingredients in the slow cook and stir to mix well.

2. Put the slow cooker lid on and cook on low for hours.

3. Fold in the pasta and green beans. Put the lid and cook on high for 20 minutes or until the vegetal are soft and the pasta is al dente.

4. Pour them in a large serving bowl and spread wi Parmesan cheese before serving.

Nutrition:

- Info Per Serving: Calories: 349;Fat: 6.7g;Protei 16.5g;Carbs: 59.9g.

Easy Bulgur Tabbouleh

Servings:4
Cooking Time:30 Minutes
Ingredients:

- 1 cucumber, peeled and chopped
- ¼ cup extra-virgin olive oil
- 8 cherry tomatoes, quartered
- 1 cup bulgur, rinsed
- 4 scallions, chopped
- ½ cup fresh parsley, chopped
- 1 lemon, juiced
- Salt and black pepper to taste

Directions:

1. Place the bulgur in a large pot with plenty of salted water, cover, and boil for 13-15 minutes. Drain and let it cool completely. Add scallions, tomatoes, cucumber, and parsley to the cooled bulgur and mix to combine. In another bowl, whisk the lemon juice, olive oil, salt, and pepper. Pour the dressing over the bulgur mixture and toss to combine. Serve.

Nutrition:

- Info Per Serving: Calories: 291;Fat: 13.7g;Protein: 7g;Carbs: 40g.

Quinoa With Baby Potatoes And Broccoli

Servings:4
Cooking Time: 10 Minutes
Ingredients:

- 2 tablespoons olive oil
- 1 cup baby potatoes, cut in half
- 1 cup broccoli florets
- 2 cups cooked quinoa
- Zest of 1 lemon
- Sea salt and freshly ground pepper, to taste

Directions:

1. Heat the olive oil in a large skillet over medium heat until shimmering.
2. Add the potatoes and cook for about 6 to 7 minutes, or until softened and golden brown. Add the broccoli and cook for about 3 minutes, or until tender.
3. Remove from the heat and add the quinoa and lemon zest. Season with salt and pepper to taste, then serve.

Nutrition:

- Info Per Serving: Calories: 205;Fat: 8.6g;Protein: 5.1g;Carbs: 27.3g.

Classic Garidomakaronada (shrimp & Pasta)

Servings:4
Cooking Time:45 Minutes
Ingredients:

- 2 tbsp olive oil
- 16 medium shrimp, shelled and deveined
- Salt and black pepper to taste
- 1 onion, finely chopped
- 3 garlic cloves, minced
- 4 tomatoes, puréed
- ½ tsp sugar
- 1 tbsp tomato paste
- 1 tbsp ouzo
- 1 lb whole-wheat spaghetti
- ½ tsp crushed red pepper
- ¼ tsp dried Greek oregano
- 2 tbsp chopped fresh parsley

Directions:

1. Bring a large pot of salted water to a boil, add the spaghetti, and cook for 7-9 minutes until al dente. Drain the pasta and set aside. Warm the olive oil in a large skillet over medium heat. Sauté the shrimp for 2 minutes, flipping once or until pink; set aside. Add the onion and garlic to the skillet and cook for 3-5 minutes or until tender.

2. Add tomatoes, sugar, oregano, and tomato paste. Bring the sauce to a boil. Reduce the heat and simmer for 15–20 minutes or until thickened. Stir in ouzo and season with salt and black pepper. Add the pasta along with crushed red pepper and cooked shrimp. Remove from heat and toss to coat the pasta. Sprinkle with parsley and serve immediately.

Nutrition:

- Info Per Serving: Calories: 319;Fat: 9g;Protein: 10g;Carbs: 51g.

Instant Pot Pork With Rice

Servings:4
Cooking Time:35 Minutes
Ingredients:

- 3 tbsp olive oil
- 1 lb pork stew meat, cubed
- Salt and black pepper to taste
- 2 chicken broth
- 1 leek, sliced
- 1 onion, chopped
- 1 carrot, sliced
- 1 cup brown rice
- 2 garlic cloves, minced
- 2 tbsp cilantro, chopped

Directions:

1. Set your Instant Pot to Sauté and heat the olive oil. Place in pork and cook for 4-5 minutes, stirring often. Add in onion, leek, garlic, and carrot and sauté for 3 more minutes. Stir in brown rice for 1 minute and pour in chicken broth; return the pork. Lock the lid in place, select Manual, and cook for 20 minutes on High. When done, do a quick pressure release. Adjust the seasoning and serve topped with cilantro.

Nutrition:

- Info Per Serving: Calories: 310;Fat: 16g;Protein: 23g;Carbs: 18g.

Lentil And Mushroom Pasta

Servings:2
Cooking Time: 50 Minutes
Ingredients:

- 2 tablespoons olive oil
- 1 large yellow onion, finely diced
- 2 portobello mushrooms, trimmed and chopped finely
- 2 tablespoons tomato paste
- 3 garlic cloves, chopped
- 1 teaspoon oregano
- 2½ cups water
- 1 cup brown lentils
- 1 can diced tomatoes with basil (with juice if diced)
- 1 tablespoon balsamic vinegar
- 8 ounces pasta of choice, cooked
- Salt and black pepper, to taste
- Chopped basil, for garnish

Directions:

1. Place a large stockpot over medium heat. Add the oil. Once the oil is hot, add the onion and mushrooms.

Cover and cook until both are soft, about 5 minutes. Add the tomato paste, garlic, and oregano and cook : minutes, stirring constantly.

2. Stir in the water and lentils. Bring to a boil, ther reduce the heat to medium-low and cook for 5 minutes covered.

3. Add the tomatoes (and juice if using diced) and vinegar. Replace the lid, reduce the heat to low and cook until the lentils are tender, about 30 minutes.

4. Remove the sauce from the heat and season with salt and pepper to taste. Garnish with the basil and serve over the cooked pasta.

Nutrition:

- Info Per Serving: Calories: 463;Fat: 15.9g;Protein 12.5g;Carbs: 70.8g.

Two-bean Cassoulet

Servings:4
Cooking Time:40 Minutes
Ingredients:

- 2 tbsp olive oil
- 1 cup canned pinto beans
- 1 cup canned can kidney beans
- 2 red bell peppers, chopped
- 1 onion, chopped
- 1 celery stalk, chopped
- 2 garlic cloves, minced
- 1 can diced tomatoes
- 1 tbsp red pepper flakes
- 1 tsp ground cumin
- Salt and black pepper to taste
- ¼ tsp ground coriander

Directions:

1. Warm olive oil in a pot over medium heat an sauté bell peppers, celery, garlic, and onion for minutes until tender. Stir in ground cumin, ground coriander, salt, and pepper for 1 minute. Pour in beans tomatoes, and red pepper flakes. Bring to a boil, then decrease the heat and simmer for another 20 minutes Serve immediately.

Nutrition:

- Info Per Serving: Calories: 361;Fat: 8.4g;Protein 17g;Carbs: 56g.

Carrot & Barley Risotto

Servings:6

Cooking Time:1 Hour 20 Minutes

Ingredients:

- 2 tbsp olive oil
- 4 cups vegetable broth
- 4 cups water
- 1 onion, chopped fine
- 1 carrot, chopped
- 1 ½ cups pearl barley
- 1 cup dry white wine
- ¼ tsp dried oregano
- 2 oz Parmesan cheese, grated
- Salt and black pepper to taste

Directions:

Bring broth and water to a simmer in a saucepan. Reduce heat to low and cover to keep warm.

Heat 1 tbsp of oil in a pot over medium heat until sizzling. Stir-fry onion and carrot until softened, 6-7 minutes. Add barley and cook, stirring often, until lightly toasted and aromatic, 4 minutes. Add wine and cook, stirring frequently for 2 minutes. Stir in 3 cups of water and oregano, bring to a simmer, and cook, stirring occasionally until liquid is absorbed, 25 minutes. Stir in 2 cups of broth, bring to a simmer, and cook until the liquid is absorbed, 15 minutes.

Continue cooking, stirring often and adding warm broth as needed to prevent the pot bottom from becoming dry until barley is cooked through but still somewhat firm in the center, 15-20 minutes. Off heat, adjust consistency with the remaining warm broth as needed. Stir in Parmesan and the remaining oil and season with salt and pepper to taste. Serve.

Nutrition:

Info Per Serving: Calories: 355;Fat: 21g;Protein: 5g;Carbs: 35g.

Black Bean & Chickpea Burgers

Servings:4

Cooking Time:35 Minutes

Ingredients:

- 1 tsp olive oil
- 1 can black beans
- 1 can chickpeas
- ½ white onion, chopped
- 2 garlic cloves, minced
- 2 free-range eggs
- 1 tsp ground cumin
- Salt and black pepper to taste
- 1 cup panko breadcrumbs
- ½ cup old-fashioned rolled oats

- 6 hamburger buns, halved
- 2 avocados
- 2 tbsp lemon juice
- 6 large lettuce leaves

Directions:

1. Preheat oven to 380 F. Blitz the black beans, chickpeas, eggs, cumin, salt, and pepper in a food processor until smooth. Transfer the mixture to a bowl and add the onion and garlic and mix well. Stir in the bread crumbs and oats. Shape the mixture into 6 balls, flatten them with your hands to make patties. Brush both sides of the burgers with oil. Arrange them on a parchment-lined baking sheet. Bake for 30 minutes, flippingonce until slightly crispy on the edges.

2. Meanwhile, mash the avocado with the lemon juice and a pinch of salt with a fork until smooth; set aside. Toast the buns for 2-3 minutes. Spread the avocado mixture onto the base of each bun, then top with the burgers and lettuce leaves. Finish with the bun tops. Serve and enjoy!

Nutrition:

- Info Per Serving: Calories: 867;Fat: 22g;Protein: 39g;Carbs: 133g.

Bulgur Pilaf With Kale And Tomatoes

Servings:2

Cooking Time: 10 Minutes

Ingredients:

- 2 tablespoons olive oil
- 2 cloves garlic, minced
- 1 bunch kale, trimmed and cut into bite-sized pieces
- Juice of 1 lemon
- 2 cups cooked bulgur wheat
- 1 pint cherry tomatoes, halved
- Sea salt and freshly ground pepper, to taste

Directions:

1. Heat the olive oil in a large skillet over medium heat. Add the garlic and sauté for 1 minute.

2. Add the kale leaves and stir to coat. Cook for 5 minutes until leaves are cooked through and thoroughly wilted.

3. Add the lemon juice, bulgur and tomatoes. Season with sea salt and freshly ground pepper to taste, then serve.

Nutrition:

- Info Per Serving: Calories: 300;Fat: 14.0g;Protein: 6.2g;Carbs: 37.8g.

Ziti Marinara Bake

Servings:4
Cooking Time:60 Minutes
Ingredients:

- For the Marinara Sauce:
- 2 tbsp olive oil
- ¼ onion, diced
- 3 cloves garlic, chopped
- 1 can tomatoes, diced
- Sprig of fresh thyme
- ½ bunch fresh basil
- Salt and pepper to taste
- For the Ziti:
- 1 lb ziti
- 3 ½ cups marinara sauce
- 1 cup cottage cheese
- 1 cup grated Mozzarella
- ¾ cup grated Pecorino cheese

Directions:

1. In a saucepan, warm the olive oil over medium heat. Stir-fry onion and garlic until lightly browned, 3 minutes. Add the tomatoes and herbs, and bring to a boil, then simmer for 7 minutes, covered. Set aside. Discard the herb sprigs and stir in sea salt and black pepper to taste.

2. Preheat the oven to 375F. Prepare the pasta according to package directions. Drain and mix the pasta in a bowl along with 2 cups of marinara sauce, cottage cheese, and half the Mozzarella and Pecorino cheeses. Transfer the mixture to a baking dish, and top with the remaining marinara sauce and cheese. Bake for 25 to 35 minutes, or until bubbly and golden brown. Serve warm.

Nutrition:

- Info Per Serving: Calories: 455;Fat: 17g;Protein: 19g;Carbs: 62g.

Papaya, Jicama, And Peas Rice Bowl

Servings:4
Cooking Time: 45 Minutes
Ingredients:

- Sauce:
- Juice of ¼ lemon
- 2 teaspoons chopped fresh basil
- 1 tablespoon raw honey
- 1 tablespoon extra-virgin olive oil
- Sea salt, to taste
- Rice:
- 1½ cups wild rice
- 2 papayas, peeled, seeded, and diced
- 1 jicama, peeled and shredded
- 1 cup snow peas, julienned
- 2 cups shredded cabbage
- 1 scallion, white and green parts, chopped

Directions:

1. Combine the ingredients for the sauce in a bow Stir to mix well. Set aside until ready to use.
2. Pour the wild rice in a saucepan, then pour enough water to cover. Bring to a boil.
3. Reduce the heat to low, then simmer for minutes or until the wild rice is soft and plump. Dra and transfer to a large serving bowl.
4. Top the rice with papayas, jicama, peas, cabbag and scallion. Pour the sauce over and stir to mix w before serving.

Nutrition:

- Info Per Serving: Calories: 446;Fat: 7.9g;Protei 13.1g;Carbs: 85.8g.

Autumn Vegetable & Rigatoni Bake

Servings:6
Cooking Time:45 Minutes
Ingredients:

- 2 tbsp grated Pecorino-Romano cheese
- 2 tbsp olive oil
- 1 lb pumpkin, chopped
- 1 zucchini, chopped
- 1 onion, chopped
- 1 lb rigatoni
- Salt and black pepper to taste
- ½ tsp garlic powder
- ½ cup dry white wine

Directions:

1. Preheat oven to 420 F. Combine zucchini, pumpk onion, and olive oil in a bowl. Arrange on a lin aluminum foil sheet and season with salt, pepper, a garlic powder. Bake for 30 minutes until tender. In pot of boiling water, cook rigatoni for 8-10 minut until al dente. Drain and set aside.

2. In a food processor, place ½ cup of the roast veggies and wine and pulse until smooth. Transfer t skillet over medium heat. Stir in rigatoni and co until heated through. Top with the remaini vegetables and Pecorino cheese to serve.

Nutrition:

- Info Per Serving: Calories: 186;Fat: 11g;Protei 10g;Carbs: 15g.

Fava And Garbanzo Bean Ful

Servings:6
Cooking Time: 10 Minutes
Ingredients:

- 1 can fava beans, rinsed and drained
- 1 can garbanzo beans, rinsed and drained
- 3 cups water
- ½ cup lemon juice
- 3 cloves garlic, peeled and minced
- 1 teaspoon salt
- 3 tablespoons extra-virgin olive oil

Directions:

1. In a pot over medium heat, cook the beans and water for 10 minutes.
2. Drain the beans and transfer to a bowl. Reserve 1 cup of the liquid from the cooked beans.
3. Add the reserved liquid, lemon juice, minced garlic and salt to the bowl with the beans. Mix to combine well. Using a potato masher, mash up about half the beans in the bowl.
4. Give the mixture one more stir to make sure the beans are evenly mixed.
5. Drizzle with the olive oil and serve.

Nutrition:

- Info Per Serving: Calories: 199;Fat: 9.0g;Protein: 10.0g;Carbs: 25.0g.

Smoky Paprika Chickpeas

Servings:4
Cooking Time:30 Minutes
Ingredients:

- ¼ cup extra-virgin olive oil
- 4 garlic cloves, sliced thin
- ½ tsp red pepper flakes
- 1 onion, chopped fine
- Salt and black pepper to taste
- 1 tsp smoked paprika
- 2 cans chickpeas
- 1 cup chicken broth
- 2 tbsp minced fresh parsley
- 2 tsp lemon juice

Directions:

1. Warm 3 tbsp of olive oil in a skillet over medium heat. Cook garlic and pepper flakes until the garlic turns golden but not brown, about 3 minutes. Stir in onion and salt and cook until softened and lightly browned, 5 minutes. Stir in smoked paprika, chickpeas,

and broth and bring to a boil. Simmer covered for 7 minutes until chickpeas are heated through.
2. Uncover, increase the heat to high, and continue to cook until nearly all liquid has evaporated, about 3 minutes. Remove and stir in parsley and lemon juice. Season with salt and pepper and drizzle with remaining olive oil. Serve warm.

Nutrition:

- Info Per Serving: Calories: 223;Fat: 11.4g;Protein: 7g;Carbs: 25g.

Pork & Garbanzo Cassoulet

Servings:4
Cooking Time:50 Minutes
Ingredients:

- 2 tbsp olive oil
- 2 lb pork stew meat, cubed
- 1 leek, chopped
- 1 red bell pepper, chopped
- 3 garlic cloves, minced
- 2 tsp sage
- 4 oz canned garbanzo beans
- 1 cup chicken stock
- 2 zucchinis, chopped
- 2 tbsp tomato paste
- 2 tbsp parsley, chopped

Directions:

1. Warm the olive oil in a pot over medium heat and sear pork meat for 10 minutes, stirring occasionally. Add in leek, bell pepper, garlic, and zucchini and sauté for 5 minutes. Stir in tomato paste and sage for 1 minute and pour in garbanzo beans and chicken stock. Cover and bring to a boil, then reduce the heat and simmer for 30 minutes. Adjust the seasoning and serve garnished with parsley.

Nutrition:

- Info Per Serving: Calories: 430;Fat: 16g;Protein: 44g;Carbs: 28g.

Chickpea Salad With Tomatoes And Basil

Servings:2
Cooking Time: 45 Minutes
Ingredients:
- 1 cup dried chickpeas, rinsed
- 1 quart water, or enough to cover the chickpeas by 3 to 4 inches
- 1½ cups halved grape tomatoes
- 1 cup chopped fresh basil leaves
- 2 to 3 tablespoons balsamic vinegar
- ½ teaspoon garlic powder
- ½ teaspoon salt, plus more as needed

Directions:
1. In your Instant Pot, combine the chickpeas and water.
2. Secure the lid. Select the Manual mode and set the cooking time for 45 minutes at High Pressure.
3. Once cooking is complete, do a natural pressure release for 20 minutes, then release any remaining pressure. Carefully open the lid and drain the chickpeas. Refrigerate to cool (unless you want to serve this warm, which is good, too).
4. While the chickpeas cool, in a large bowl, stir together the basil, tomatoes, vinegar, garlic powder, and salt. Add the beans, stir to combine, and serve.

Nutrition:
- Info Per Serving: Calories: 395;Fat: 6.0g;Protein: 19.8g;Carbs: 67.1g.

Florentine Bean & Vegetable Gratin

Servings:4
Cooking Time:50 Minutes
Ingredients:
- ½ cup Parmigiano Reggiano cheese, grated
- 4 pancetta slices
- 2 tbsp olive oil
- 4 garlic cloves, minced
- 1 onion, chopped
- ½ fennel bulb, chopped
- 1 tbsp brown rice flour
- 2 cans white beans
- 1 can tomatoes, diced
- 1 medium zucchini, chopped
- 1 tsp porcini powder
- 1 tbsp fresh basil, chopped
- ½ tsp dried oregano
- 1 tsp red pepper flakes

- Salt to taste
- 2 tbsp butter, cubed

Directions:
1. Heat the olive in a skillet over medium heat. Fr the pancetta for 5 minutes until crispy. Drain on pape towels, chop, and reserve. Add garlic, onion, and fenne to the skillet and sauté for 5 minutes until softened Stir in rice flour for 3 minutes.
2. Preheat oven to 350 F. Add the beans, tomatoe and zucchini to a casserole dish and pour in th sautéed vegetable and chopped pancetta; mix well Sprinkle with porcini powder, oregano, red peppe flakes, and salt. Top with Parmigiano Reggiano chees and butter and bake for 25 minutes or until the chees is lightly browned. Garnish with basil and serve.

Nutrition:
- Info Per Serving: Calories: 483;Fat: 28g;Protein 19g;Carbs: 42g.

Spanish-style Linguine With Tapenade

Servings:4
Cooking Time:20 Minutes
Ingredients:
- 1 cup black olives, pitted
- 2 tbsp capers
- 2 tbsp rosemary, chopped
- 1 garlic clove, smashed
- 2 anchovy fillets, chopped
- ½ tsp sugar
- ⅔ cup + 2 tbsp olive oil
- 1 lb linguine
- ½ cup grated Manchego cheese
- 1 tbsp chopped fresh chives

Directions:
1. Process the olives, capers, rosemary, garlic anchovies, sugar, and ⅔ cup olive oil in your foo processor until well incorporated but not smooth; se aside. Bring a large pot of salted water to a boil, add th linguine, and cook for 7-9 minutes until al dente. Drai the pasta in a bowl and add the remaining tablespoons olive oil and Manchego cheese; toss to coa Arrange pasta on a serving platter and top it wit tapenade and chives. Serve and enjoy!

Nutrition:
- Info Per Serving: Calories: 375;Fat: 39g;Protein 5g;Carbs: 23g.

Pesto Fusilli With Broccoli

Servings:4
Cooking Time:25 Minutes
Ingredients:

    ¼ cup olive oil

    4 Roma tomatoes, diced

    1 cup broccoli florets

    1 lb fusilli

    2 tsp tomato paste

    2 garlic cloves, minced

    1 tbsp chopped fresh oregano

    ½ tsp salt

    1 cup vegetable broth

    6 fresh basil leaves

    ¼ cup grated Parmesan cheese

    ¼ cup pine nuts

Directions:

Place the pasta in a pot with salted boiling water and cook for 8-10 minutes until al dente. Drain and set aside. In a pan over medium heat, sauté tomato paste, tomatoes, broth, oregano, garlic, and salt for 10 minutes.

In a food processor, place basil, broccoli, Parmesan, olive oil, and pine nuts; pulse until smooth. Pour into the tomato mixture. Stir in pasta, cook until heated through and the pasta is well coated. Serve.

Nutrition:

Info Per Serving: Calories: 385;Fat: 22g;Protein: 2g;Carbs: 38g.

Creamy Mussel Spaghetti

Servings:4
Cooking Time:20 Minutes
Ingredients:

    1 lb mussels, debearded and rinsed

    2 tbsp olive oil

    16 oz spaghetti, broken in half

    1 cup white wine

    3 shallots, finely chopped

    6 garlic cloves, minced

    2 tsp red chili flakes

    ½ cup fish stock

    1 ½ cups heavy cream

    2 tbsp chopped fresh parsley

    Salt and black pepper to taste

Directions:

1. Boil water in a pot over medium heat and place in the pasta. Cook for 8-10 minutes for al dente. Drain and set aside.

2. Pour mussels and white wine into a pot, cover, and cook for 4 minutes. Occasionally stir until the mussels have opened. Strain the mussels and reserve the cooking liquid. Allow cooling, discard any mussels with closed shells, and remove the meat out of ¾ of the mussel shells. Set aside the remaining mussels in the shells.

3. Heat olive oil in a skillet and sauté shallots, garlic, and chili flakes for 3 minutes. Mix in reduced wine and fish stock. Allow boiling and whisk in the heavy cream. Taste the sauce and adjust the seasoning with salt and pepper; top with parsley. Pour in the pasta, mussels and toss well in the sauce.

Nutrition:

• Info Per Serving: Calories: 471;Fat: 34g;Protein: 19g;Carbs: 19g.

Mushroom & Green Onion Rice Pilaf

Servings:4
Cooking Time:30 Minutes
Ingredients:

• 2 tbsp olive oil

• 1 cup rice, rinsed

• 2 greens onions, chopped

• 2 cups chicken stock

• 1 cup mushrooms, sliced

• 1 garlic clove, minced

• Salt and black pepper to taste

• ½ cup Parmesan cheese, grated

• 2 tbsp cilantro, chopped

Directions:

1. Warm the olive oil in a skillet over medium heat and cook onion, garlic, and mushrooms for 5 minutes until tender. Stir in rice, salt, and pepper for 1 minute. Pour in chicken stock and cook for 15-18 minutes. Transfer to a platter, scatter Parmesan cheese all over, and sprinkle with cilantro to serve.

Nutrition:

• Info Per Serving: Calories: 250;Fat: 10g;Protein: 13g;Carbs: 28g.

Ribollita (tuscan Bean Soup)

Servings:6
Cooking Time:1 Hour 45 Minutes

Ingredients:

- 3 tbsp olive oil
- Salt and black pepper to taste
- 2 cups canned cannellini beans
- 6 oz pancetta, chopped
- ¼ tsp red pepper flakes
- 1 onion, chopped
- 2 carrots, chopped
- 1 celery rib, chopped
- 3 garlic cloves, minced
- 4 cups chicken broth
- 1 lb lacinato kale, chopped
- 1 can diced tomatoes
- 1 rosemary sprig, chopped
- Crusty bread for serving

Directions:

1. Warm the olive oil in a skillet over medium heat and add the pancetta. Cook, stirring occasionally, until pancetta is lightly browned and fat has rendered, 5-6 minutes. Add onion, carrots, and celery and cook, stirring occasionally, until softened and lightly browned, 4-6 minutes. Stir in garlic and red pepper flakes and cook until fragrant, 1 minute.

2. Stir in broth, 2 cups of water, and beans and bring to a boil. Cover and simmer for 15 minutes. Stir in lacinato kale and tomatoes and cook for another 5 minutes. Sprinkle with rosemary and adjust the taste. Serve with crusty bread.

Nutrition:

- Info Per Serving: Calories: 385;Fat: 18g;Protein: 36g;Carbs: 25g.

Lush Moroccan Chickpea, Vegetable, And Fruit Stew

Servings:6

Cooking Time: 6 Hours 4 Minutes

Ingredients:

- 1 large bell pepper, any color, chopped
- 6 ounces green beans, trimmed and cut into bit size pieces
- 3 cups canned chickpeas, rinsed and drained
- 1 can diced tomatoes, with the juice
- 1 large carrot, cut into ¼-inch rounds
- 2 large potatoes, peeled and cubed
- 1 large yellow onion, chopped
- 1 teaspoon grated fresh ginger
- 2 garlic cloves, minced
- 1¾ cups low-sodium vegetable soup
- 1 teaspoon ground cumin
- 1 tablespoon ground coriander
- ¼ teaspoon ground red pepper flakes
- Sea salt and ground black pepper, to taste
- 8 ounces fresh baby spinach
- ¼ cup diced dried figs
- ¼ cup diced dried apricots
- 1 cup plain Greek yogurt

Directions:

1. Place the bell peppers, green beans, chicken pea tomatoes and juice, carrot, potatoes, onion, ginger, a garlic in the slow cooker.

2. Pour in the vegetable soup and sprinkle with cum coriander, red pepper flakes, salt, and ground bla pepper. Stir to mix well.

3. Put the slow cooker lid on and cook on high for hours or until the vegetables are soft. Stir periodically

4. Open the lid and fold in the spinach, figs, aprico and yogurt. Stir to mix well.

5. Cook for 4 minutes or until the spinach is wilte Pour them in a large serving bowl. Allow to cool for least 20 minutes, then serve warm.

Nutrition:

- Info Per Serving: Calories: 611;Fat: 9.0g;Protei 30.7g;Carbs: 107.4g.

Sides , Salads, And Soups Recipes

Green Salad With Lentils & Feta Cheese

Servings:4
Cooking Time:25 Min + Cooling Time
Ingredients:

- 2 tbsp olive oil
- 1 head broccoli, cut into florets
- 1 lb baby spinach
- 2 green onions, sliced
- 1 garlic clove, minced
- 1 cup brown lentils
- Salt and black pepper to taste
- ½ tsp sweet paprika
- ½ tsp ginger, grated
- ¼ cup lemon juice
- ¾ cup feta cheese, crumbled

Directions:

1. Blanch the broccoli in salted water in a pot over medium heat for 3-4 minutes. Drain and set aside to cool.
2. Warm the olive oil in the pot and cook green onions and garlic for 3 minutes. Pour in lentils and cover with water. Simmer covered for 15-20 minutes. Drain and let it cool.
3. In a bowl, whisk lemon juice, salt, pepper, sweet paprika, and ginger. Divide the baby spinach between four salad plates, top with lentils and broccoli and drizzle with the prepared dressing. Sprinkle with feta cheese and serve topped.

Nutrition:

- Info Per Serving: Calories: 300;Fat: 4g;Protein: 22g;Carbs: 50g.

Traditional Dukkah Spice

Servings:6
Cooking Time:50 Minutes
Ingredients:

- ⅓ cup black sesame seeds, toasted
- 1 tsp olive oil
- 1 can chickpeas
- ½ cup almonds, toasted
- 2 tbsp coriander seeds
- 1 tbsp cumin seeds, toasted
- 2 tsp fennel seeds, toasted
- Salt and black pepper to taste

Directions:

1. Preheat oven to 400 F. Spread the chickpeas in a single layer on a baking sheet and drizzle with olive oil. Roast for 40-45 minutes until browned and crisp, stirring every 5-10 minutes. Remove and let cool completely.
2. Blend the remaining ingredients in your food processor and remove to a bowl. Pour the cooled chickpeas into the food processor and pulse until coarsely ground. Mix them with the almonds and seeds until well combined. Store the spices in an airtight container at room temperature for up to 1 month.

Nutrition:

- Info Per Serving: Calories: 198;Fat: 3.0g;Protein: 2.1g;Carbs: 5g.

Bell Pepper & Chickpea Salad

Servings:4
Cooking Time:40 Min + Chilling Time
Ingredients:

- 1 cup chickpeas, soaked
- 1 cucumber, sliced
- 10 cherry tomatoes, halved
- 1 red bell peppers, sliced
- 1 green bell pepper, sliced
- 1 tsp yellow mustard
- 1 tsp coriander seeds
- ½ hot banana pepper, minced
- 1 tbsp fresh lemon juice
- 1 tbsp balsamic vinegar
- 2 tbsp olive oil
- Salt and black pepper to taste
- 2 tbsp fresh cilantro, chopped
- 2 tbsp capers

Directions:

1. Cover the chickpeas with water by 2 inches in a pot over medium heat. Bring it to a boil. Turn the heat to a simmer and continue to cook for about 40 minutes or until tender. Drain, let cool and transfer to a salad bowl. Add in the remaining ingredients and toss to combine well. Serve.

Nutrition:

- Info Per Serving: Calories: 470;Fat: 13g;Protein: 22g;Carbs: 73g.

Orange Pear Salad With Gorgonzola

Servings:4
Cooking Time:10 Minutes
Ingredients:
- 4 oz gorgonzola cheese, crumbled
- 2 tbsp olive oil
- 1 tsp orange zest
- ¼ cup orange juice
- 3 tbsp balsamic vinegar
- Salt and black pepper to taste
- 1 romaine lettuce head, torn
- 2 pears, cored and cut into medium wedges

Directions:
1. Mix orange zest, orange juice, vinegar, oil, salt, pepper, lettuce, pears, and gorgonzola cheese in a bowl. Serve.

Nutrition:
- Info Per Serving: Calories: 210;Fat: 6g;Protein: 4g;Carbs: 11g.

Tuscan-style Panzanella Salad

Servings:4
Cooking Time:25 Minutes
Ingredients:
- 2 cups mixed cherry tomatoes, quartered
- 4 bread slices, crusts removed, cubed
- 4 tbsp extra-virgin olive oil
- 1 cucumber, sliced
- ½ red onion, thinly sliced
- ¼ cup chopped fresh basil
- ½ tsp dried oregano
- 1 tbsp capers
- 1 garlic clove, minced
- ¼ cup red wine vinegar
- 2 anchovy fillets, chopped
- Salt and black pepper to taste

Directions:
1. Preheat oven to 320 F. Pour the bread cubes into a baking dish and drizzle with 2 tbsp of olive oil. Bake for 6-8 minutes, shaking occasionally until browned and crisp. Let cool. Toss the cooled bread, cherry tomatoes, cucumber, red onion, basil, anchovies, and capers in a serving dish.
2. In another bowl, whisk the remaining olive oil, oregano, red wine vinegar, and garlic. Adjust the seasoning with salt and pepper. Drizzle the dressing over the salad and toss to coat.

Nutrition:
- Info Per Serving: Calories: 228;Fat: 21.6g;Protein 2g;Carbs: 8.2g.

Vegetable Fagioli Soup

Servings:2
Cooking Time: 60 Minutes
Ingredients:
- 1 tablespoon olive oil
- 2 medium carrots, diced
- 2 medium celery stalks, diced
- ½ medium onion, diced
- 1 large garlic clove, minced
- 3 tablespoons tomato paste
- 4 cups low-sodium vegetable broth
- 1 cup packed kale, stemmed and chopped
- 1 can red kidney beans, drained and rinsed
- 1 can cannellini beans, drained and rinsed
- ½ cup chopped fresh basil
- Salt and freshly ground black pepper, to taste

Directions:
1. Heat the olive oil in a stockpot over medium-high heat. Add the carrots, celery, onion, and garlic an sauté for 10 minutes, or until the vegetables start t turn golden.
2. Stir in the tomato paste and cook for about 3 seconds.
3. Add the vegetable broth and bring the soup to boil. Cover, and reduce the heat to low. Cook the sou for 45 minutes, or until the carrots are tender.
4. Using an immersion blender, purée the soup s that it's partly smooth, but with some chunks c vegetables.
5. Add the kale, beans, and basil. Season with salt an pepper to taste, then serve.

Nutrition:
- Info Per Serving: Calories: 217;Fat: 4.2g;Protein 10.0g;Carbs: 36.2g.

Cheesy Roasted Broccolini

Servings:2

Cooking Time: 10 Minutes

Ingredients:

1 bunch broccolini

1 tablespoon olive oil

½ teaspoon garlic powder

¼ teaspoon salt

2 tablespoons grated Romano cheese

Directions:

Preheat the oven to 400°F. Line a sheet pan with parchment paper.

. Slice the tough ends off the broccolini and put in a medium bowl. Add the olive oil, garlic powder, and salt and toss to coat well. Arrange the broccolini on the prepared sheet pan.

. Roast in the preheated oven for 7 minutes, flipping halfway through the cooking time.

. Remove the pan from the oven and sprinkle the cheese over the broccolini. Using tongs, carefully flip the broccolini over to coat all sides.

. Return to the oven and cook for an additional 2 to minutes, or until the cheese melts and starts to turn golden. Serve warm.

Nutrition:

Info Per Serving: Calories: 114;Fat: 9.0g;Protein: 0g;Carbs: 5.0g.

Mushroom & Spinach Orzo Soup

Servings:4

Cooking Time:20 Minutes

Ingredients:

2 tbsp butter

3 cups spinach

½ cup orzo

4 cups chicken broth

1 cup feta cheese, crumbled

Salt and black pepper to taste

½ tsp dried oregano

1 onion, chopped

2 garlic cloves, minced

1 cup mushrooms, sliced

Directions:

Melt butter in a pot over medium heat and sauté onion, garlic, and mushrooms for 5 minutes until tender. Add in chicken broth, orzo, salt, pepper, and oregano. Bring to a boil and reduce the heat to a low. Continue simmering for 10 minutes, partially covered.

Stir in spinach and continue to cook until the spinach wilts, about 3-4 minutes. Ladle into individual bowls and serve garnished with feta cheese.

Nutrition:

• Info Per Serving: Calories: 370;Fat: 11g;Protein: 23g;Carbs: 44g.

Mixed Salad With Balsamic Honey Dressing

Servings:2

Cooking Time: 0 Minutes

Ingredients:

• Dressing:

• ¼ cup balsamic vinegar

• ¼ cup olive oil

• 1 tablespoon honey

• 1 teaspoon Dijon mustard

• ¼ teaspoon garlic powder

• ¼ teaspoon salt, or more to taste

• Pinch freshly ground black pepper

• Salad:

• 4 cups chopped red leaf lettuce

• ½ cup cherry or grape tomatoes, halved

• ½ English cucumber, sliced in quarters lengthwise and then cut into bite-size pieces

• Any combination fresh, torn herbs (parsley, oregano, basil, or chives)

• 1 tablespoon roasted sunflower seeds

Directions:

1. Make the Dressing

2. Combine the vinegar, olive oil, honey, mustard, garlic powder, salt, and pepper in a jar with a lid. Shake well.

3. Make the Salad

4. In a large bowl, combine the lettuce, tomatoes, cucumber, and herbs. Toss well.

5. Pour all or as much dressing as desired over the tossed salad and toss again to coat the salad with dressing.

6. Top with the sunflower seeds before serving.

Nutrition:

• Info Per Serving: Calories: 337;Fat: 26.1g;Protein: 4.2g;Carbs: 22.2g.

Andalusian Lentil Soup

Servings:4
Cooking Time:25 Minutes
Ingredients:
- 2 tbsp olive oil
- 3 cups vegetable broth
- 1 cup tomato sauce
- 1 onion, chopped
- 1 cup dry red lentils
- ½ cup prepared salsa verde
- 2 garlic cloves, minced
- 1 tbsp smoked paprika
- 2 tsp ground cumin
- ¼ tsp cayenne pepper
- Salt and black pepper to taste
- 2 tbsp crushed tortilla chips

Directions:
1. Warm the olive oil on Sauté in your Instant Pot. Stir in garlic and onion and cook for 5 minutes until golden brown. Add in tomato sauce, broth, salsa verde, cumin, cayenne pepper, lentils, paprika, salt, and pepper. Seal the lid and cook for 20 minutes on High Pressure. Release pressure naturally for 10 minutes. Top with crushed tortilla chips and serve.

Nutrition:
- Info Per Serving: Calories: 324;Fat: 10g;Protein: 14g;Carbs: 47g.

Rice Stuffed Bell Peppers

Servings:4
Cooking Time:70 Minutes
Ingredients:
- 4 red bell peppers, tops and seeds removed
- 2 tbsp olive oil
- 1 cup cooked brown rice
- 4 oz crumbled feta cheese
- 4 cups fresh baby spinach
- 3 Roma tomatoes, chopped
- 1 onion, finely chopped
- 1 cup mushrooms, sliced
- 2 garlic cloves, minced
- 1 tsp dried oregano
- Salt and black pepper to taste
- 2 tbsp fresh parsley, chopped

Directions:
1. Preheat oven to 350 F. Warm olive oil in a skillet over medium heat and sauté onion, garlic, and mushrooms for 5 minutes. Stir in tomatoes, spinach, rice, salt, oregano, parsley, and pepper, cook for minutes until the spinach wilts. Remove from the hea Stuff the bell peppers with the rice mixture and t with feta cheese. Arrange the peppers on a greas baking pan and pour in 1/4 cup of water. Bake cover with aluminum foil for 30 minutes. Then, ba uncovered for another 10 minutes. Serve and enjoy!

Nutrition:
- Info Per Serving: Calories: 387;Fat: 15g;Prote 12g;Carbs: 55g.

Sumptuous Greek Vegetable Salad

Servings:6
Cooking Time: 0 Minutes
Ingredients:
- Salad:
- 1 can chickpeas, drained and rinsed
- 1 can artichoke hearts, drained and halved
- 1 head Bibb lettuce, chopped
- 1 cucumber, peeled deseeded, and chopped
- 1½ cups grape tomatoes, halved
- ¼ cup chopped basil leaves
- ½ cup sliced black olives
- ½ cup cubed feta cheese
- Dressing:
- 1 tablespoon freshly squeezed lemon juice (fro about ½ small lemon)
- ¼ teaspoon freshly ground black pepper
- 1 tablespoon chopped fresh oregano
- 2 tablespoons extra-virgin olive oil
- 1 tablespoon red wine vinegar
- 1 teaspoon honey

Directions:
1. Combine the ingredients for the salad in a lar salad bowl, then toss to combine well.
2. Combine the ingredients for the dressing in a sm bowl, then stir to mix well.
3. Dressing the salad and serve immediately.

Nutrition:
- Info Per Serving: Calories: 165;Fat: 8.1g;Prote 7.2g;Carbs: 17.9g.

Cabbage & Turkey Soup

Servings:4
Cooking Time:40 Minutes
Ingredients:

- 2 tbsp olive oil
- ½ lb turkey breast, cubed
- 2 leeks, sliced
- 4 spring onions, chopped
- 2 cups green cabbage, grated
- 4 celery sticks, chopped
- 4 cups vegetable stock
- ½ tsp sweet paprika
- ½ tsp ground nutmeg
- Salt and black pepper to taste

Directions:
1. Warm the olive oil in a pot over medium heat and brown turkey for 4 minutes, stirring occasionally. Add in leeks, spring onions, and celery and cook for another minute. Stir in cabbage, vegetable stock, sweet paprika, nutmeg, salt, and pepper and bring to a boil. Cook for 30 minutes. Serve.

Nutrition:
- Info Per Serving: Calories: 320;Fat: 16g;Protein: 19g;Carbs: 25g.

Chorizo & Fire-roasted Tomato Soup

Servings:4
Cooking Time:25 Minutes
Ingredients:

- 28 oz fire-roasted diced tomatoes
- 1 tbsp olive oil
- 2 shallots, chopped
- 3 cloves garlic, minced
- Salt and black pepper to taste
- 4 cups beef broth
- ½ cup fresh ripe tomatoes
- 1 tbsp red wine vinegar
- 3 chorizo sausage, chopped
- ½ cup thinly chopped basil

Directions:
1. Warm the olive oil on Sauté in your Instant Pot. Cook the chorizo until crispy, stirring occasionally, about 5 minutes. Remove to a plate. Add the garlic and shallots to the pot and sauté for 3 minutes until soft. Season with salt and pepper.

2. Stir in red wine vinegar, broth, diced tomatoes, and ripe tomatoes. Seal the lid and cook on High Pressure for 8 minutes. Release the pressure quickly. Pour the soup into a blender and process until smooth. Divide into bowls, top with chorizo, and decorate with basil.

Nutrition:
- Info Per Serving: Calories: 771;Fat: 27g;Protein: 40g;Carbs: 117g.

Grilled Bell Pepper And Anchovy Antipasto

Servings:4
Cooking Time: 8 Minutes
Ingredients:

- 2 tablespoons extra-virgin olive oil, divided
- 4 medium red bell peppers, quartered, stem and seeds removed
- 6 ounces anchovies in oil, chopped
- 2 tablespoons capers, rinsed and drained
- 1 cup Kalamata olives, pitted
- 1 small shallot, chopped
- Sea salt and freshly ground pepper, to taste

Directions:
1. Heat the grill to medium-high heat. Grease the grill grates with 1 tablespoon of olive oil.
2. Arrange the red bell peppers on the preheated grill grates, then grill for 8 minutes or until charred.
3. Turn off the grill and allow the pepper to cool for 10 minutes.
4. Transfer the charred pepper in a colander. Rinse and peel the peppers under running cold water, then pat dry with paper towels.
5. Cut the peppers into chunks and combine with remaining ingredients in a large bowl. Toss to mix well.
6. Serve immediately.

Nutrition:
- Info Per Serving: Calories: 227;Fat: 14.9g;Protein: 13.9g;Carbs: 9.9g.

Lebanese Crunchy Salad With Seeds

Servings:4
Cooking Time:15 Minutes
Ingredients:
- For the Salad
- 1 head Romaine lettuce, separated into leaves
- 1 cup sunflower seeds, toasted
- 1 Lebanese cucumber, sliced
- 1 tbsp cilantro, chopped
- 2 tbsp black olives, pitted
- 8 cherry tomatoes, halved
- For Dressing
- 1 lemon, juiced
- ½ tsp Mediterranean herb mix
- 2 tbsp onions, chopped
- ½ tsp paprika
- ½ tsp garlic, chopped
- Salt and black pepper to taste

Directions:
1. Toss all of the salad ingredients in a bowl. Whisk all of the dressing ingredients until creamy and smooth. Dress your salad and serve.

Nutrition:
- Info Per Serving: Calories: 210;Fat: 16g;Protein: 8g;Carbs: 7g.

Italian-style Chicken Stew

Servings:4
Cooking Time:20 Minutes
Ingredients:
- 2 fire-roasted tomatoes, peeled, chopped
- 2 lb chicken wings
- 2 potatoes, peeled and chopped
- 1 carrot, chopped
- 2 garlic cloves, chopped
- 2 tbsp olive oil
- 1 tsp smoked paprika, ground
- 4 cups chicken broth
- 2 tbsp fresh parsley, chopped
- Salt and black pepper to taste
- 1 cup spinach, chopped

Directions:
1. Preheat your Instant Pot on Sauté mode. Rub the chicken with salt, pepper, and paprika, and place in the pot. Stir in all remaining ingredients. Seal the lid and cook on High Pressure for 8 minutes. When ready, do quick release.

Nutrition:
- Info Per Serving: Calories: 626;Fat: 26g;Protein 74g;Carbs: 23g.

Greek Chicken, Tomato, And Olive Salad

Servings:2
Cooking Time: 0 Minutes
Ingredients:
- Salad:
- 2 grilled boneless, skinless chicken breasts, sliced
- 10 cherry tomatoes, halved
- 8 pitted Kalamata olives, halved
- ½ cup thinly sliced red onion
- Dressing:
- ¼ cup balsamic vinegar
- 1 teaspoon freshly squeezed lemon juice
- ¼ teaspoon sea salt
- ¼ teaspoon freshly ground black pepper
- 2 teaspoons extra-virgin olive oil
- For Serving:
- 2 cups roughly chopped romaine lettuce
- ½ cup crumbled feta cheese

Directions:
1. Combine the ingredients for the salad in a large bowl. Toss to combine well.
2. Combine the ingredients for the dressing in a small bowl. Stir to mix well.
3. Pour the dressing the bowl of salad, then toss t coat well. Wrap the bowl in plastic and refrigerate fc at least 2 hours.
4. Remove the bowl from the refrigerator. Spread th lettuce on a large plate, then top with marinated salad Scatter the salad with feta cheese and serv immediately.

Nutrition:
- Info Per Serving: Calories: 328;Fat: 16.9g;Protein 27.6g;Carbs: 15.9g.

Root Veggie Soup

Servings:4
Cooking Time:40 Minutes
Ingredients:

3 cups chopped butternut squash

2 tbsp olive oil

1 carrot, chopped

1 leek, chopped

2 garlic cloves, minced

1 celery stalk, chopped

1 parsnip, chopped

1 potato, chopped

4 cups vegetable broth

1 tsp dried thyme

Salt and black pepper to taste

Directions:

Warm olive oil in a pot over medium heat and sauté leek, garlic, parsnip, carrot, and celery for 5-6 minutes until the veggies start to brown. Throw in squash, potato, broth, thyme, salt, and pepper. Bring to boil, then decrease the heat and simmer for 20-30 minutes until the veggies soften. Transfer to a food processor and blend until you get a smooth and homogeneous consistency.

Nutrition:

Info Per Serving: Calories: 200;Fat: 9g;Protein: 2g;Carbs: 25.8g.

Cheese & Broccoli Quiche

Servings:4
Cooking Time:45 Minutes
Ingredients:

1 tsp Mediterranean seasoning

3 eggs

½ cup heavy cream

3 tbsp olive oil

1 red onion, chopped

2 garlic cloves, minced

2 oz mozzarella, shredded

1 lb broccoli, cut into florets

Directions:

Preheat oven to 320 F. Warm the oil in a pan over medium heat. Sauté the onion and garlic until just tender and fragrant. Add in the broccoli and continue to cook until crisp-tender for about 4 minutes. Spoon the mixture into a greased casserole dish. Beat the eggs with heavy cream and Mediterranean seasoning. Spoon this mixture over the broccoli layer. Bake for 18-20 minutes. Top with the shredded cheese and broil for 5 to 6 minutes or until hot and bubbly on the top. Serve.

Nutrition:

• Info Per Serving: Calories: 198;Fat: 14g;Protein: 5g;Carbs: 12g.

Bell Pepper & Lentil Salad With Tomatoes

Servings:4
Cooking Time:10 Minutes
Ingredients:

• 2 tomatoes, chopped

• 1 green bell pepper, chopped

• 14 oz canned lentils, drained

• 2 spring onions, chopped

• 1 red bell pepper, chopped

• 2 tbsp cilantro, chopped

• 2 tsp balsamic vinegar

Directions:

1. Mix lentils, spring onions, tomatoes, bell peppers, cilantro, and vinegar in a bowl. Serve immediately.

Nutrition:

• Info Per Serving: Calories: 210;Fat: 3g;Protein: 7g;Carbs: 12g.

Favorite Green Bean Stir-fry

Servings:4
Cooking Time:15 Minutes
Ingredients:

• 1 tbsp olive oil

• 1 tbsp butter

• 1 fennel bulb, sliced

• 1 red onion, sliced

• 4 cloves garlic, pressed

• 1 lb green beans, steamed

• ½ tsp dried oregano

• 2 tbsp balsamic vinegar

• Salt and black pepper to taste

Directions:

1. Heat the butter and olive oil a saucepan over medium heat. Add in the onion and garlic and sauté for 3 minutes. Stir in oregano, fennel, balsamic vinegar, salt, and pepper. Stir-fry for another 6-8 minutes and add in the green beans; cook for 2-3 minutes. Adjust the seasoning and serve.

Nutrition:

• Info Per Serving: Calories: 126;Fat: 6g;Protein: 3.3g;Carbs: 16.6g.

Authentic Marinara Sauce

Servings:6
Cooking Time:46 Minutes
Ingredients:

- 2 cans crushed tomatoes with their juices
- 1 tsp dried oregano
- 2 tbsp + ¼ cup olive oil
- 2 tbsp butter
- 1 small onion, diced
- 1 red bell pepper, chopped
- 4 garlic cloves, minced
- Salt and black pepper to taste
- ½ cup thinly sliced basil
- 2 tbsp chopped rosemary
- 1 tsp red pepper flakes

Directions:

1. Warm 2 tablespoons olive oil and butter in a large skillet over medium heat. Add the onion, garlic, and red pepper and sauté for about 5 minutes until tender. Season with salt and pepper. Reduce the heat to low and add the tomatoes and their juices, remaining olive oil, oregano, half of the basil, rosemary, and red pepper flakes. Bring to a simmer and cover. Cook for 50-60 minutes. Blitz the sauce with an immersion blender and sprinkle with the remaining basil.

Nutrition:

- Info Per Serving: Calories: 265;Fat: 19g;Protein: 4.1g;Carbs: 18g.

Greek-style Pasta Salad

Servings:4
Cooking Time:10 Minutes
Ingredients:

- 2 tbsp olive oil
- 16 oz fusilli pasta
- 1 yellow bell pepper, cubed
- 1 green bell pepper, cubed
- Salt to taste
- 3 tomatoes, cubed
- 1 red onion, sliced
- 2 cups feta cheese, crumbled
- ¼ cup lemon juice
- 1 tbsp lemon zest, grated
- 1 cucumber, cubed
- 1 cup Kalamata olives, sliced

Directions:

1. Cook the fusilli pasta in boiling salted water until "al dente", 8-10 minutes. Drain and set aside to cool. In a bowl, whisk together olive oil, lemon zest, lemon juice, and salt. Add in bell peppers, tomatoes, onion, feta cheese, cucumber, olives, and pasta and toss to combine. Serve.

Nutrition:

- Info Per Serving: Calories: 420;Fat: 18g;Protein 15g;Carbs: 50g.

Moroccan Chicken & Chickpea Stew

Servings:6
Cooking Time:40 Minutes
Ingredients:

- 1 lb boneless, skinless chicken legs
- 2 tsp ground cumin
- ½ tsp cayenne pepper
- 2 tbsp olive oil
- 1 onion, minced
- 2 jalapeño peppers, minced
- 3 garlic cloves, crushed
- 2 tsp freshly grated ginger
- ¼ cup chicken stock
- 1 can diced tomatoes
- 2 cans chickpeas
- Salt to taste
- ½ cup coconut milk
- ¼ cup fresh parsley, chopped
- 2 cups cooked basmati rice

Directions:

1. Season the chicken with salt, cayenne pepper, and cumin. Set on Sauté and warm the oil. Add in jalapeño peppers and onion, and cook for 5 minutes. Mix ginger and garlic, and cook for 3 minutes until tender.
2. Add ¼ cup chicken stock into the cooker and scrape any browned bits of food. Mix the onion mixture with chickpeas, tomatoes, and salt. Stir Seasoned chicken to coat in sauce.
3. Seal the lid and cook on High Pressure for minutes. Release the pressure quickly. Remove the chicken and slice into chunks. Into the remaining sauce mix in coconut milk; simmer for 5 minutes on Keep Warm. Split rice into 4 bowls. Top with chicken, then sauce and add cilantro for garnish.

Nutrition:

- Info Per Serving: Calories: 996;Fat: 24g;Protein 55g;Carbs: 143g.

Root Vegetable Roast

Servings:4

Cooking Time: 25 Minutes

Ingredients:

- 1 bunch beets, peeled and cut into 1-inch cubes
- 2 small sweet potatoes, peeled and cut into 1-inch cubes
- 3 parsnips, peeled and cut into 1-inch rounds
- 4 carrots, peeled and cut into 1-inch rounds
- 1 tablespoon raw honey
- 1 teaspoon sea salt
- ½ teaspoon freshly ground black pepper
- 1 tablespoon extra-virgin olive oil
- 2 tablespoons coconut oil, melted

Directions:

1. Preheat the oven to 400°F. Line a baking sheet with parchment paper.

2. Combine all the ingredients in a large bowl. Toss to coat the vegetables well.

3. Pour the mixture in the baking sheet, then place the sheet in the preheated oven.

4. Roast for 25 minutes or until the vegetables are lightly browned and soft. Flip the vegetables halfway through the cooking time.

5. Remove the vegetables from the oven and allow to cool before serving.

Nutrition:

- Info Per Serving: Calories: 461;Fat: 18.1g;Protein: 5.9g;Carbs: 74.2g.

Cherry & Pine Nut Couscous

Servings:6

Cooking Time:10 Minutes

Ingredients:

- 2 tbsp olive oil
- 3 cups hot water
- 1 cup couscous
- ½ cup pine nuts, roasted
- ½ cup dry cherries, chopped
- ½ cup parsley, chopped
- Salt and black pepper to taste
- 1 tbsp lime juice

Directions:

1. Place couscous and hot water in a bowl and let sit for 10 minutes. Fluff with a fork and remove to a bowl. Stir in pine nuts, cherries, parsley, salt, pepper, lime juice, and olive oil.

Nutrition:

- Info Per Serving: Calories: 220;Fat: 8g;Protein: 6g;Carbs: 9g.

Olive Tapenade Flatbread With Cheese

Servings:4

Cooking Time:35 Min + Chilling Time

Ingredients:

- For the flatbread
- 2 tbsp olive oil
- 2 ½ tsp dry yeast
- 1 ½ cups all-purpose flour
- ¾ tsp salt
- ½ cup lukewarm water
- ¼ tsp sugar
- For the tapenade
- 2 roasted red pepper slices, chopped
- ¼ cup extra-virgin olive oil
- 1 cup green olives, chopped
- 10 black olives, chopped
- 1 tbsp capers
- 1 garlic clove, minced
- 1 tbsp chopped basil leaves
- 1 tbsp chopped fresh oregano
- ¼ cup goat cheese, crumbled

Directions:

1. Combine lukewarm water, sugar, and yeast in a bowl. Set aside covered for 5 minutes. Mix the flour and salt in a bowl. Pour in the yeast mixture and mix. Knead until you obtain a ball. Place the dough onto a floured surface and knead for 5 minutes until soft. Leave the dough into an oiled bowl, covered to rise until it has doubled in size, about 40 minutes.

2. Preheat oven to 400 F. Cut the dough into 4 balls and roll each one out to a ½ inch thickness. Bake for 5 minutes. In a blender, mix black olives, roasted pepper, green olives, capers, garlic, oregano, basil, and olive oil for 20 seconds until coarsely chopped. Spread the olive tapenade on the flatbreads and top with goat cheese to serve.

Nutrition:

- Info Per Serving: Calories: 366;Fat: 19g;Protein: 7.3g;Carbs: 42g.

Brussels Sprout And Apple Slaw

Servings:4
Cooking Time: 0 Minutes
Ingredients:

* Salad:
* 1 pound Brussels sprouts, stem ends removed and sliced thinly
* 1 apple, cored and sliced thinly
* ½ red onion, sliced thinly
* Dressing:
* 1 teaspoon Dijon mustard
* 2 teaspoons apple cider vinegar
* 1 tablespoon raw honey
* 1 cup plain coconut yogurt
* 1 teaspoon sea salt
* For Garnish:
* ½ cup pomegranate seeds
* ½ cup chopped toasted hazelnuts

Directions:

1. Combine the ingredients for the salad in a large salad bowl, then toss to combine well.
2. Combine the ingredients for the dressing in a small bowl, then stir to mix well.
3. Dressing the salad. Let sit for 30 minutes, then serve with pomegranate seeds and toasted hazelnuts on top.

Nutrition:

* Info Per Serving: Calories: 248;Fat: 11.2g;Protein: 12.7g;Carbs: 29.9g.

Radish & Pecorino Salad

Servings:6
Cooking Time:15 Minutes
Ingredients:

* 6 tbsp grated Pecorino Romano cheese
* ¼ cup extra-virgin olive oil
* 6 cups kale, chopped
* 2 tbsp lemon juice
* Salt to taste
* 2 cups arugula
* ⅓ cup shelled pistachios
* 20 radishes, sliced

Directions:

1. In a salad bowl, whisk the olive oil, lemon juice, and salt. Add the kale and gently massage the leaves with your hands for about 15 seconds until all are thoroughly coated. Let the kale sit for 5 minutes. Add in the arugula, radishes, and pistachios and toss. Sprinkle with Pecorino and serve.

Nutrition:

* Info Per Serving: Calories: 105;Fat: 9.2g;Protein 4g;Carbs: 3.8g.

Beef Stew With Veggies

Servings:6
Cooking Time:75 Minutes
Ingredients:

* ¼ cup flour
* 1 tsp paprika
* 1 tsp ground black pepper
* 2 lb beef chuck, cubed
* 2 tbsp olive oil
* 2 tbsp butter
* 1 onion, diced
* 3 garlic cloves, minced
* 1 cup dry red wine
* 2 cups beef stock
* 1 tbsp dried Italian Seasoning
* 2 tsp Worcestershire sauce
* 4 cups potatoes, diced
* 2 celery stalks, chopped
* 3 cups carrots, chopped
* 3 tomatoes, chopped
* 2 bell peppers, chopped
* Salt and black pepper to taste
* 2 tbsp fresh parsley, chopped

Directions:

1. Preheat your Instant Pot on Sauté mode. In a bow mix black pepper, beef, flour, paprika, and salt. Tos the ingredients and ensure the beef is wel coated. Warm the butter and oil in the pot, add in mea and cook for 8- 10 minutes until browned. Set aside. T the same fat, add garlic, onion, and celery, bell peppe and cook for 4-5 minutes until tender.
2. Deglaze with wine, scrape the bottom to get rid o any browned beef bits. Pour in beef stoc Worcestershire sauce, and Italian seasoning. Retur beef to the pot; add carrots, tomatoes, and potatoe Seal the lid, press Meat/Stew and cook on Hig Pressure for 35 minutes. Release Pressure naturally fo 10 minutes. Taste and adjust the seasonings a necessary. Serve on plates and scatter over the parsley

Nutrition:

* Info Per Serving: Calories: 548;Fat: 19g;Protei 51g;Carbs: 35g.

Sautéed White Beans With Rosemary

Servings:2
Cooking Time: 12 Minutes
Ingredients:

- 1 tablespoon olive oil
- 2 garlic cloves, minced
- 1 can white cannellini beans, drained and rinsed
- 1 teaspoon minced fresh rosemary plus 1 whole fresh rosemary sprig
- ¼ teaspoon dried sage
- ½ cup low-sodium chicken stock
- Salt, to taste

Directions:

Heat the olive oil in a saucepan over medium-high heat.

Add the garlic and sauté for 30 seconds until fragrant.

Add the beans, minced and whole rosemary, sage, and chicken stock and bring the mixture to a boil.

Reduce the heat to medium and allow to simmer for 10 minutes, or until most of the liquid is evaporated.

If desired, mash some of the beans with a fork to thicken them.

Season with salt to taste. Remove the rosemary sprig before serving.

Nutrition:

- Info Per Serving: Calories: 155;Fat: 7.0g;Protein: 0g;Carbs: 17.0g.

Minty Bulgur With Fried Halloumi

Servings:4
Cooking Time:35 Minutes
Ingredients:

- 2 tbsp olive oil
- 4 halloumi cheese slices
- 1 cup bulgur
- 1 cup parsley, chopped
- ¼ cup mint, chopped
- 3 tbsp lemon juice
- 1 red onion, sliced
- Salt and black pepper to taste

Directions:

Bring to a boil a pot of water over medium heat. Add in bulgur and simmer for 15 minutes. Drain and let it cool in a bowl. Stir in parsley, mint, lemon juice, onion, salt, and pepper. Warm half of olive oil in a pan over medium heat. Cook the halloumi for 4-5 minutes on both sides until golden. Arrange the fried cheese on top of the bulgur and serve.

Nutrition:

- Info Per Serving: Calories: 330;Fat: 12g;Protein: 28g;Carbs: 31g.

Red Cabbage Coleslaw With Almonds

Servings:4
Cooking Time:10 Minutes
Ingredients:

- 2 tbsp olive oil
- 1 head red cabbage, shredded
- 2 tbsp cilantro, chopped
- ½ cup almonds, chopped
- 1 tomato, cubed
- Salt and black pepper to taste
- 1 tbsp white wine vinegar

Directions:

1. Mix red cabbage, cilantro, almonds, olive oil, tomato, salt, pepper, and vinegar in a bowl. Serve cold.

Nutrition:

- Info Per Serving: Calories: 220;Fat: 7g;Protein: 9g;Carbs: 7g.

Black Olive & Radish Salad

Servings:4
Cooking Time:10 Minutes
Ingredients:

- 2 tbsp olive oil
- 1 Romaine lettuce, shredded
- 1 lb red radishes, sliced
- 1 tbsp lemon zest
- Salt and black pepper to taste
- 2 tbsp parsley, chopped
- 1 small red onion, sliced
- 10 black olives, sliced

Directions:

1. Mix lemon zest, salt, pepper, parsley, olive oil, radishes, onion, olives, and lettuce in a bowl. Serve right away.

Nutrition:

- Info Per Serving: Calories: 80;Fat: 5g;Protein: 3g;Carbs: 4g.

Roasted Root Vegetable Soup

Servings:6
Cooking Time: 35 Minutes
Ingredients:

- 2 parsnips, peeled and sliced
- 2 carrots, peeled and sliced
- 2 sweet potatoes, peeled and sliced
- 1 teaspoon chopped fresh rosemary
- 1 teaspoon chopped fresh thyme
- 1 teaspoon sea salt
- ½ teaspoon freshly ground black pepper
- 2 tablespoons extra-virgin olive oil
- 4 cups low-sodium vegetable soup
- ½ cup grated Parmesan cheese, for garnish (optional)

Directions:

1. Preheat the oven to 400°F. Line a baking sheet with aluminum foil.
2. Combine the parsnips, carrots, and sweet potatoes in a large bowl, then sprinkle with rosemary, thyme, salt, and pepper, and drizzle with olive oil. Toss to coat the vegetables well.
3. Arrange the vegetables on the baking sheet, then roast in the preheated oven for 30 minutes or until lightly browned and soft. Flip the vegetables halfway through the roasting.
4. Pour the roasted vegetables with vegetable broth in a food processor, then pulse until creamy and smooth.
5. Pour the puréed vegetables in a saucepan, then warm over low heat until heated through.
6. Spoon the soup in a large serving bowl, then scatter with Parmesan cheese. Serve immediately.

Nutrition:

- Info Per Serving: Calories: 192;Fat: 5.7g;Protein: 4.8g;Carbs: 31.5g.

Simple Mushroom Barley Soup

Servings:6
Cooking Time: 20 To 23 Minutes
Ingredients:

- 2 tablespoons extra-virgin olive oil
- 1 cup chopped carrots
- 1 cup chopped onion
- 5½ cups chopped mushrooms
- 6 cups no-salt-added vegetable broth
- 1 cup uncooked pearled barley
- ¼ cup red wine
- 2 tablespoons tomato paste

- 4 sprigs fresh thyme or ½ teaspoon dried thyme
- 1 dried bay leaf
- 6 tablespoons grated Parmesan cheese

Directions:

1. In a large stockpot over medium heat, heat the o Add the onion and carrots and cook for 5 minute stirring frequently. Turn up the heat to medium-hi; and add the mushrooms. Cook for 3 minutes, stirri frequently.
2. Add the broth, barley, wine, tomato paste, thyn and bay leaf. Stir, cover, and bring the soup to a bc Once it's boiling, stir a few times, reduce the heat medium-low, cover, and cook for another 12 to minutes, until the barley is cooked through.
3. Remove the bay leaf and serve the soup in bov with 1 tablespoon of cheese sprinkled on top of each.

Nutrition:

- Info Per Serving: Calories: 195;Fat: 4.0g;Prote 7.0g;Carbs: 34.0g.

Broccoli & Garlic Stir Fry

Servings:4
Cooking Time:15 Minutes
Ingredients:

- 1 red bell pepper, cut into chunks
- 3 tbsp olive oil
- 2 garlic cloves, minced
- ½ tsp red pepper flakes
- ½ lb broccoli florets
- Salt to taste
- 2 tsp lemon juice
- 1 tbsp anchovy paste

Directions:

1. Warm the olive oil in a skillet over medium he Add the broccoli, garlic, and red pepper flakes and s briefly for 3-4 minutes until the florets turn brig green. Season with salt. Add 2 tbsp of water and broccoli cook for another 2–3 minutes. Stir in the r bell pepper, lemon juice, and anchovy paste and co for 1 more minute. Serve immediately.

Nutrition:

- Info Per Serving: Calories: 114;Fat: 11g;Prote 3g;Carbs: 4g.

Kale & Chicken Soup With Vermicelli

Servings:4
Cooking Time:25 Minutes
Ingredients:

- 2 tbsp olive oil
- 1 carrot, chopped
- 1 leek, chopped
- ½ cup vermicelli
- 4 cups chicken stock
- 2 cups kale, chopped
- 2 chicken breasts, cubed
- 1 cup orzo
- ¼ cup lemon juice
- 2 tbsp parsley, chopped
- Salt and black pepper to taste

Directions:
1. Warm the olive oil in a pot over medium heat and sauté leek and chicken for 6 minutes. Stir in carrot and chicken stock and bring to a boil. Cook for 10 minutes. Add in vermicelli, kale, orzo, and lemon juice and continue cooking for another 5 minutes. Adjust the seasoning with salt and pepper and sprinkle with parsley. Ladle into soup bowls and serve.

Nutrition:
- Info Per Serving: Calories: 310;Fat: 13g;Protein: 3g;Carbs: 17g.

Roasted Cherry Tomato & Fennel

Servings:4
Cooking Time:35 Minutes
Ingredients:

- ¼ cup olive oil
- 20 cherry tomatoes, halved
- 2 fennel bulbs, cut into wedges
- 10 black olives, sliced
- 1 lemon, cut into wedges
- Salt and black pepper to taste

Directions:
1. Preheat oven to 425 F. Combine fennel, olive oil, tomatoes, salt, and pepper in a bowl. Place in a baking pan and roast in the oven for about 25 minutes until golden. Top with olives and serve with lemon wedges on the side.

Nutrition:
- Info Per Serving: Calories: 268;Fat: 15.2g;Protein: g;Carbs: 33g.

Feta & Cannellini Bean Soup

Servings:4
Cooking Time:30 Minutes
Ingredients:

- 2 tbsp olive oil
- 4 oz feta cheese, crumbled
- 1 cup collard greens, torn
- 2 cups canned cannellini beans
- 1 fennel bulb, chopped
- 1 carrot, chopped
- ½ cup spring onions, chopped
- ½ tsp dried rosemary
- ½ tsp dried basil
- 1 garlic clove, minced
- 4 cups vegetable broth
- 2 tbsp tomato paste
- Salt and black pepper to taste

Directions:
1. In a pot over medium heat, warm the olive oil. Add in fennel, garlic, carrot, and spring onions and sauté until tender, about 2-3 minutes. Stir in tomato paste, rosemary, and basil and cook for 2 more minutes. Pour in vegetable broth and cannellini beans. Bring to a boil, then lower the heat, and simmer for 15 minutes. Add in collard greens and cook for another 2-3 minutes until wilted. Adjust the seasoning with salt and pepper. Top with feta cheese and serve.

Nutrition:
- Info Per Serving: Calories: 519;Fat: 15g;Protein: 32g;Carbs: 65g.

Lemony Yogurt Sauce

Servings:4
Cooking Time:5 Minutes
Ingredients:

- 1 cup plain yogurt
- 1 tbsp fresh chives, chopped
- ½ lemon, zested and juiced
- 1 garlic clove, minced
- Salt and black pepper to taste

Directions:
1. Place the yogurt, lemon zest and juice, and garlic in a bowl and mix well. Season with salt and pepper. Let sit for about 30 minutes to blend the flavors. Store in an airtight container in the refrigerator for up to 2-3 days. Serve topped with chives.

Nutrition:
- Info Per Serving: Calories: 258;Fat: 8g;Protein: 8.9g;Carbs: 12.9g.

Leek & Shrimp Soup

Servings:6
Cooking Time:40 Minutes
Ingredients:

- 1 lb shrimp, peeled and deveined
- 3 tbsp olive oil
- 1 celery stalk, chopped
- 1 leek, sliced
- 1 fennel bulb, chopped
- 2 garlic cloves, minced
- Salt and black pepper to taste
- 1 tbsp coriander seeds
- 6 cups vegetable broth
- 2 tbsp buttermilk
- 1 lemon, juiced

Directions:

1. Warm the oil in a large pot oven over medium heat. Add the celery, leek, and fennel, and cook for about 5 minutes until tender. Add the garlic and season with salt and pepper. Add the coriander seeds and stir. Pour in the broth, bring to a boil, and then reduce to a simmer and cook for 20 more minutes. Add the shrimp to the soup and cook until just pink, about 3 minutes. Stir in buttermilk and lemon juice. Serve.

Nutrition:

- Info Per Serving: Calories: 286;Fat: 9g;Protein: 17g;Carbs: 34g.

Tasty Cucumber & Couscous Salad

Servings:4
Cooking Time:30 Minutes
Ingredients:

- ¼ cup olive oil
- 2 tbsp balsamic vinegar
- 1 cup couscous
- 1 cucumber, sliced
- Salt and black pepper to taste
- 2 tbsp lemon juice

Directions:

1. Place couscous in a bowl with 3 cups of hot water and let sit for 10 minutes. Fluff with a fork and remove to a bowl. Stir in cucumber, salt, pepper, lemon juice, vinegar, and olive oil. Serve immediately.

Nutrition:

- Info Per Serving: Calories: 180;Fat: 6g;Protein: 5g;Carbs: 12g.

Anchovy Salad With Mustard Vinaigrette

Servings:6
Cooking Time:10 Minutes
Ingredients:

- ½ cup olive oil
- ½ lemon, juiced
- 1 tsp Dijon mustard
- ¼ tsp honey
- Salt and black pepper to taste
- 4 tomatoes, diced
- 1 cucumber, peeled and diced
- 1 lb arugula
- 1 red onion, thinly sliced
- 2 tbsp parsley, chopped
- 4 anchovy filets, chopped

Directions:

1. In a bowl, whisk together the olive oil, lemon juice, honey, and mustard, and season with salt and pepper. Set aside. In a separate bowl, combine all the vegetables with the parsley and toss. Add the sardine fillets on top of the salad. Drizzle the dressing over the salad just before serving.

Nutrition:

- Info Per Serving: Calories: 168;Fat: 6g;Protein: 8g;Carbs: 29g.

Pesto Ravioli Salad

Servings:6
Cooking Time:15 Minutes
Ingredients:

- 1 cup smoked mozzarella cheese, cubed
- ¼ tsp lemon zest
- 1 cup basil pesto
- ½ cup mayonnaise
- 2 red bell peppers, chopped
- 18 oz cheese ravioli

Directions:

1. Bring to a boil salted water in a pot over high heat. Add the ravioli and cook, uncovered, for 4-5 minutes, stirring occasionally; drain and place them in a salad bowl to cool slightly. Blend the lemon zest, pesto, and mayonnaise in a large bowl and stir in mozzarella cheese and bell peppers. Pour the mixture over the ravioli and toss to coat. Serve.

Nutrition:

- Info Per Serving: Calories: 447;Fat: 32g;Protein: 18g;Carbs: 24g.

Moroccan Zucchini & Lentil Soup

Servings:6
Cooking Time:30 Minutes
Ingredients:

- 2 tbsp olive oil
- 1 onion, diced
- 3 garlic cloves, minced
- 1 tsp cinnamon
- 1 tsp ground cumin
- 1 tsp ground coriander
- 1 can tomatoes, diced
- 6 cups vegetable stock
- 1 ½ cups green lentils
- 1 carrot, chopped
- 1 zucchini, diced
- ½ tsp dried thyme
- Salt and black pepper to taste
- 1 tbsp fresh mint, chopped

Directions:

Warm the olive oil in a large stockpot over medium heat. Sauté the onions and garlic just until tender and translucent, 3 minutes. Stir in cinnamon, cumin, ground coriander, thyme, salt, and pepper for 30 seconds. Pour in the vegetable stock and bring to a boil, stirring frequently. Add the lentils and carrot and simmer for 15 minutes. Add the zucchini and cook for 5 minutes or until the zucchini is tender. Spoon into individual bowls and top with fresh mint.

Nutrition:

Info Per Serving: Calories: 243;Fat: 8g;Protein: ;Carbs: 29g.

Sweet Chickpea & Mushroom Stew

Servings:4
Cooking Time:20 Minutes
Ingredients:

- ½ tbsp button mushrooms, chopped
- 1 cup chickpeas, cooked
- 1 onion, peeled, chopped
- 1 lb string beans, trimmed
- 1 apple, cut into 1-inch cubes
- ½ cup raisins
- 2 carrots, chopped
- 2 garlic cloves, crushed
- 4 cherry tomatoes
- 2 tbsp fresh mint, chopped
- 1 tsp grated ginger
- ½ cup orange juice
- ½ tsp salt

Directions:
1. Place all ingredients in the instant pot. Pour enough water to cover. Cook on High Pressure for 8 minutes. Do a natural release for 10 minutes.
Nutrition:
- Info Per Serving: Calories: 350;Fat: 3.7g;Protein: 14g;Carbs: 71g.

Lemon And Spinach Orzo

Servings:2
Cooking Time: 10 Minutes
Ingredients:

- 1 cup dry orzo
- 1 bag baby spinach
- 1 cup halved grape tomatoes
- 2 tablespoons extra-virgin olive oil
- ¼ teaspoon salt
- Freshly ground black pepper
- ¾ cup crumbled feta cheese
- 1 lemon, juiced and zested

Directions:
1. Bring a medium pot of water to a boil. Stir in the orzo and cook uncovered for 8 minutes. Drain the water, then return the orzo to medium heat.
2. Add the spinach and tomatoes and cook until the spinach is wilted.
3. Sprinkle with the olive oil, salt, and pepper and mix well. Top with the feta cheese, lemon juice and zest, then toss one or two more times and serve.
Nutrition:
- Info Per Serving: Calories: 610;Fat: 27.0g;Protein: 21.0g;Carbs: 74.0g.

Parsley Carrot & Cabbage Salad

Servings:4
Cooking Time:10 Minutes
Ingredients:

- 2 tbsp olive oil
- 1 green cabbage head, torn
- 1 tbsp lemon juice
- 1 carrot, grated
- Salt and black pepper to taste
- ¼ cup parsley, chopped

Directions:
1. Mix olive oil, lemon juice, carrot, parsley, salt, pepper, and cabbage in a bowl. Serve right away.
Nutrition:
- Info Per Serving: Calories: 110;Fat: 5g;Protein: 5g;Carbs: 5g.

Parmesan Roasted Red Potatoes

Servings:2

Cooking Time: 55 Minutes

Ingredients:

- 12 ounces red potatoes, scrubbed and diced into 1-inch pieces
- 1 tablespoon olive oil
- ½ teaspoon garlic powder
- ¼ teaspoon salt
- 1 tablespoon grated Parmesan cheese
- 1 teaspoon minced fresh rosemary

Directions:

1. Preheat the oven to 425°F. Line a baking sheet with parchment paper.

2. In a mixing bowl, combine the potatoes, olive oil, garlic powder, and salt. Toss well to coat.

3. Lay the potatoes on the parchment paper and roast for 10 minutes. Flip the potatoes over and roast for another 10 minutes.

4. Check the potatoes to make sure they are golden brown on the top and bottom. Toss them again, turn the heat down to 350°F, and roast for 30 minutes more.

5. When the potatoes are golden brown, scatter the Parmesan cheese over them and toss again. Return to the oven for 3 minutes to melt the cheese.

6. Remove from the oven and sprinkle with the fresh rosemary before serving.

Nutrition:

- Info Per Serving: Calories: 200;Fat: 8.2g;Protein: 5.1g;Carbs: 30.0g.

Arugula And Fig Salad

Servings:2

Cooking Time: 0 Minutes

Ingredients:

- 3 cups arugula
- 4 fresh, ripe figs, stemmed and sliced
- 2 tablespoons olive oil
- ¼ cup lightly toasted pecan halves
- 2 tablespoons crumbled blue cheese
- 1 to 2 tablespoons balsamic glaze

Directions:

1. Toss the arugula and figs with the olive oil in a large bowl until evenly coated.

2. Add the pecans and blue cheese to the bowl. Toss the salad lightly.

3. Drizzle with the balsamic glaze and serve immediately.

Nutrition:

- Info Per Serving: Calories: 517;Fat: 36.2g;Protei 18.9g;Carbs: 30.2g.

Classic Potato Salad With Green Onions

Servings:4

Cooking Time:25 Minutes

Ingredients:

- 2 ½ lb baby potatoes, halved
- Salt and black pepper to taste
- 1 cup light mayonnaise
- Juice of 1 lemon
- 2 green onions, chopped
- ¼ cup parsley, chopped

Directions:

1. Place potatoes and enough water in a pot ov medium heat and bring to a boil. Cook for 12 minut and drain; set aside.

2. In a bowl, mix mayonnaise, salt, pepper, lem juice, and green onions. Add in the baby potatoes a toss to coat. Top with parsley and serve immediately.

Nutrition:

- Info Per Serving: Calories: 360;Fat: 20g;Prote 11g;Carbs: 25g.

Balsamic Watermelon & Feta Salad

Servings:2

Cooking Time:10 Minutes

Ingredients:

- 3 cups packed arugula
- 2 ½ cups watermelon, cubed
- 2 oz feta cheese, crumbled
- 2 tbsp balsamic glaze
- 1 tsp mint leaves, chopped

Directions:

1. Place the arugula on a salad plate. Top w watermelon cubes and sprinkle with feta chee Drizzle the balsamic glaze all over and garnish w chopped mint leaves. Serve.

Nutrition:

- Info Per Serving: Calories: 159;Fat: 7.2g;Prote 6.1g;Carbs: 21g.

North African Tomato & Pepper Salad

Servings:6
Cooking Time:20 Minutes
Ingredients:

- 4 tbsp olive oil
- 2 green bell peppers
- 1 jalapeño pepper
- 4 tomatoes, peeled and diced
- 1 cucumber, peeled and diced
- 1 tbsp dill, chopped
- 1 tbsp parsley, chopped
- 1 tsp ground cumin
- 1 lemon, juiced
- Salt and black pepper to taste

Directions:

1. Preheat oven to 360 F. Bake the bell peppers and jalapeño until the skin blackens and blisters. Combine the rest of the ingredients in a medium bowl and mix well. Remove the skins of the peppers. Seed and chop the peppers and add them to the salad. Season with salt and ground pepper. Toss to combine and serve.

Nutrition:

- Info Per Serving: Calories: 179;Fat: 10g;Protein: 4g;Carbs: 31g.

Fish And Seafood Recipes

Grilled Lemon Pesto Salmon

Servings:2
Cooking Time: 6 To 10 Minutes
Ingredients:

- 10 ounces salmon fillet
- Salt and freshly ground black pepper, to taste
- 2 tablespoons prepared pesto sauce
- 1 large fresh lemon, sliced
- Cooking spray

Directions:

1. Preheat the grill to medium-high heat. Spray the grill grates with cooking spray.
2. Season the salmon with salt and black pepper. Spread the pesto sauce on top.
3. Make a bed of fresh lemon slices about the same size as the salmon fillet on the hot grill, and place the salmon on top of the lemon slices. Put any additional lemon slices on top of the salmon.
4. Grill the salmon for 6 to 10 minutes, or until the fish is opaque and flakes apart easily.
5. Serve hot.

Nutrition:

- Info Per Serving: Calories: 316;Fat: 21.1g;Protein: 29.0g;Carbs: 1.0g.

Baked Halibut With Eggplants

Servings:4
Cooking Time:35 Minutes
Ingredients:

- 2 tbsp olive oil
- ¼ cup tomato sauce
- 4 halibut fillets, boneless
- 2 eggplants, sliced
- Salt and black pepper to taste
- 2 tbsp balsamic vinegar
- 2 tbsp chives, chopped

Directions:

1. Preheat the oven to 380F. Warm the olive oil in a skillet over medium heat and fry the eggplant slices for 5-6 minutes, turning once; reserve. Add the tomato sauce, salt, pepper, and vinegar to the skillet and cook for 5 minutes. Return the eggplants to the skillet and cook for 2 minutes. Remove to a plate. Place the halibut fillets on a greased baking tray and bake for 12-15 minutes. Serve the halibut over the eggplants sprinkled with chives.

Nutrition:

- Info Per Serving: Calories: 300;Fat: 13g;Protein: 16g;Carbs: 19g.

Balsamic-honey Glazed Salmon

Servings:4
Cooking Time: 8 Minutes
Ingredients:

- ½ cup balsamic vinegar
- 1 tablespoon honey
- 4 salmon fillets
- Sea salt and freshly ground pepper, to taste
- 1 tablespoon olive oil

Directions:

1. Heat a skillet over medium-high heat. Combine the vinegar and honey in a small bowl.
2. Season the salmon fillets with the sea salt and freshly ground pepper; brush with the honey-balsamic glaze.
3. Add olive oil to the skillet, and sear the salmon fillets, cooking for 3 to 4 minutes on each side until lightly browned and medium rare in the center.
4. Let sit for 5 minutes before serving.

Nutrition:

- Info Per Serving: Calories: 454;Fat: 17.3g;Protein: 65.3g;Carbs: 9.7g.

Drunken Mussels With Lemon-butter Sauce

Servings:4
Cooking Time:15 Minutes
Ingredients:

- 4 lb mussels, cleaned
- 4 tbsp butter
- ½ cup chopped parsley
- 1 white onion, chopped
- 2 cups dry white wine
- ½ tsp sea salt
- 6 garlic cloves, minced
- Juice of ½ lemon

Directions:

1. Add wine, garlic, salt, onion, and ¼ cup of parsley in a pot over medium heat and let simmer. Put in mussels and simmer covered for 7-8 minutes. Divide mussels between four bowls. Stir butter and lemon juice into the pot and drizzle over the mussels. Top with parsley and serve.

Nutrition:

- Info Per Serving: Calories: 487;Fat: 18g;Protein: 37g;Carbs: 26g.

Italian Tilapia Pilaf

Servings:2
Cooking Time:45 Minutes
Ingredients:

- 3 tbsp olive oil
- 2 tilapia fillets, boneless
- ½ tsp Italian seasoning
- ½ cup brown rice
- ½ cup green bell pepper, diced
- ½ cup white onions, chopped
- ½ tsp garlic powder
- Salt and black pepper to taste

Directions:

1. Warm 1 tbsp of olive oil in a saucepan ove medium heat. Cook onions, bell pepper, garlic powde Italian seasoning, salt, and pepper for 3 minutes. Sti in brown rice and 2 cups of water and bring to simmer. Cook for 18 minutes. Warm the remaining o in a skillet over medium heat. Season the tilapia wit salt and pepper. Fry for 10 minutes on both side Share the rice among plates and top with the tilapi fillets.

Nutrition:

- Info Per Serving: Calories: 270;Fat: 18g;Protei 13g;Carbs: 26g.

Pancetta-wrapped Scallops

Servings:6
Cooking Time:25 Minutes
Ingredients:

- 2 tsp olive oil
- 12 thin pancetta slices
- 12 medium scallops
- 2 tsp lemon juice
- 1 tsp chili powder

Directions:

1. Wrap pancetta around scallops and secure wit toothpicks. Warm the olive oil in a skillet over mediu heat and cook scallops for 6 minutes on all sides. Serv sprinkled with chili powder and lemon juice.

Nutrition:

- Info Per Serving: Calories: 310;Fat: 25g;Protei 19g;Carbs: 24g.

Baked Halibut Steaks With Vegetables

Servings:4

Cooking Time: 20 Minutes

Ingredients:

- 2 teaspoon olive oil, divided
- 1 clove garlic, peeled and minced
- ½ cup minced onion
- 1 cup diced zucchini
- 2 cups diced fresh tomatoes
- 2 tablespoons chopped fresh basil
- ¼ teaspoon salt
- ¼ teaspoon ground black pepper
- 4 halibut steaks
- ⅓ cup crumbled feta cheese

Directions:

Preheat oven to 450°F. Coat a shallow baking dish lightly with 1 teaspoon of olive oil.

In a medium saucepan, heat the remaining 1 teaspoon of olive oil.

Add the garlic, onion, and zucchini and mix well. Cook for 5 minutes, stirring occasionally, or until the zucchini is softened.

Remove the saucepan from the heat and stir in the tomatoes, basil, salt, and pepper.

Place the halibut steaks in the coated baking dish in a single layer. Spread the zucchini mixture evenly over the steaks. Scatter the top with feta cheese.

Bake in the preheated oven for about 15 minutes, or until the fish flakes when pressed lightly with a fork. Serve hot.

Nutrition:

Info Per Serving: Calories: 258;Fat: 7.6g;Protein: 3.6g;Carbs: 6.5g.

Dill Chutney Salmon

Servings:2

Cooking Time: 3 Minutes

Ingredients:

Chutney:

- ¼ cup fresh dill
- ¼ cup extra virgin olive oil
- Juice from ½ lemon
- Sea salt, to taste

Fish:

- 2 cups water
- 2 salmon fillets

- Juice from ½ lemon
- ¼ teaspoon paprika
- Salt and freshly ground pepper to taste

Directions:

1. Pulse all the chutney ingredients in a food processor until creamy. Set aside.

2. Add the water and steamer basket to the Instant Pot. Place salmon fillets, skin-side down, on the steamer basket. Drizzle the lemon juice over salmon and sprinkle with the paprika.

3. Secure the lid. Select the Manual mode and set the cooking time for 3 minutes at High Pressure.

4. Once cooking is complete, do a quick pressure release. Carefully open the lid.

5. Season the fillets with pepper and salt to taste. Serve topped with the dill chutney.

Nutrition:

- Info Per Serving: Calories: 636;Fat: 41.1g;Protein: 65.3g;Carbs: 1.9g.

Pan-seared Trout With Tzatziki

Servings:4

Cooking Time:20 Minutes

Ingredients:

- 1 cucumber, grated and squeezed
- 3 tbsp olive oil
- 4 trout fillets, boneless
- ½ lime, juiced
- Salt and black pepper to taste
- 1 garlic clove, minced
- 1 tsp sweet paprika
- 4 garlic cloves, minced
- 2 cups Greek yogurt
- 1 tbsp dill, chopped

Directions:

1. Warm 2 tbsp of the olive oil in a skillet over medium heat. Sprinkle the trout with salt, pepper, lime juice, garlic, and paprika and sear for 8 minutes on all sides. Remove to a paper towel–lined plate. Combine cucumber, garlic, remaining olive oil, yogurt, salt, and dill in a bowl. Share trout into plates and serve with tzatziki.

Nutrition:

- Info Per Serving: Calories: 400;Fat: 19g;Protein: 41g;Carbs: 19g.

Shrimp & Gnocchi With Feta Cheese

Servings:4
Cooking Time:30 Minutes
Ingredients:

- 1 lb shrimp, shells and tails removed
- 1 jar roasted red peppers, chopped
- 2 tbsp olive oil
- 1 cup chopped fresh tomato
- 2 garlic cloves, minced
- ½ tsp dried oregano
- Black pepper to taste
- ¼ tsp crushed red peppers
- 1 lb potato gnocchi
- ½ cup cubed feta cheese
- ⅓ cup fresh basil leaves, torn

Directions:

1. Preheat oven to 425 F. In a baking dish, mix the tomatoes, olive oil, garlic, oregano, black pepper, and crushed red peppers. Roast in the oven for 10 minutes. Stir in the roasted peppers and shrimp. Roast for 10 minutes until the shrimp turn pink. Bring a saucepan of salted water to the boil and cook the gnocchi for 1-2 mins, until floating. Drain. Remove the dish from the oven. Mix in the cooked gnocchi, sprinkle with feta and basil and serve.

Nutrition:

- Info Per Serving: Calories: 146;Fat: 5g;Protein: 23g;Carbs: 1g.

Spiced Citrus Sole

Servings:4
Cooking Time: 10 Minutes
Ingredients:

- 1 teaspoon garlic powder
- 1 teaspoon chili powder
- ½ teaspoon lemon zest
- ½ teaspoon lime zest
- ¼ teaspoon smoked paprika
- ¼ teaspoon freshly ground black pepper
- Pinch sea salt
- 4 sole fillets, patted dry
- 1 tablespoon extra-virgin olive oil
- 2 teaspoons freshly squeezed lime juice

Directions:

1. Preheat the oven to 450ºF. Line a baking sheet with aluminum foil and set aside.

2. Mix together the garlic powder, chili powder, lemon zest, lime zest, paprika, pepper, and salt in a small bowl until well combined.

3. Arrange the sole fillets on the prepared baking sheet and rub the spice mixture all over the fillets until well coated. Drizzle the olive oil and lime juice over the fillets.

4. Bake in the preheated oven for about 8 minutes until flaky.

5. Remove from the heat to a plate and serve.

Nutrition:

- Info Per Serving: Calories: 183;Fat: 5.0g;Protein: 32.1g;Carbs: 0g.

Roman-style Cod

Servings:2
Cooking Time:40 Minutes
Ingredients:

- 2 cod fillets, cut in 4 portions
- ¼ tsp paprika
- ¼ tsp onion powder
- 3 tbsp olive oil
- 4 medium scallions
- 2 tbsp fresh chopped basil
- 3 tbsp minced garlic
- Salt and black pepper to taste
- ¼ tsp dry marjoram
- 6 sun-dried tomato slices
- ½ cup dry white wine
- ½ cup ricotta cheese, crumbled
- 1 can artichoke hearts
- 1 lemon, sliced
- 1 cup pitted black olives
- 1 tsp capers

Directions:

1. Preheat oven to 375 F. Warm the olive oil in a skillet over medium heat. Sprinkle the cod with paprika and onion powder. Sear it for about 1 minute per side or until golden; reserve. Add the scallions, basil, garlic, salt, pepper, marjoram, tomatoes, and wine to the same skillet. Bring to a boil. Remove the skillet from the heat. Arrange the fish on top of the sauce and sprinkle with ricotta cheese.

2. Place the artichokes in the pan and top with lemon slices. Sprinkle with black olives and capers. Place the skillet in the oven. Bake for 15-20 minutes until flakes easily with a fork.

Nutrition:

- Info Per Serving: Calories: 1172;Fat: 59g;Protein: 64g;Carbs: 94g.

Slow Cooker Salmon In Foil

Servings:2

Cooking Time: 2 Hours

Ingredients:

- 2 salmon fillets
- 1 tablespoon olive oil
- 2 cloves garlic, minced
- ½ tablespoon lime juice
- 1 teaspoon finely chopped fresh parsley
- ¼ teaspoon black pepper

Directions:

1. Spread a length of foil onto a work surface and place the salmon fillets in the middle.

2. Mix together the olive oil, garlic, lime juice, parsley, and black pepper in a small bowl. Brush the mixture over the fillets. Fold the foil over and crimp the sides to make a packet.

3. Place the packet into the slow cooker, cover, and cook on High for 2 hours, or until the fish flakes easily with a fork.

4. Serve hot.

Nutrition:

- Info Per Serving: Calories: 446;Fat: 20.7g;Protein: 65.4g;Carbs: 1.5g.

Crispy Sole Fillets

Servings:4

Cooking Time:10 Minutes

Ingredients:

- ¼ cup olive oil
- ½ cup flour
- ½ tsp paprika
- 8 skinless sole fillets
- Salt and black pepper to taste
- 4 lemon wedges

Directions:

Warm the olive oil in a skillet over medium heat. Mix the flour with paprika in a shallow dish. Coat the fish with the flour, shaking off any excess. Sear the sole fillets for 2-3 minutes per side until lightly browned. Serve with lemon wedges.

Nutrition:

Info Per Serving: Calories: 219;Fat: 15g;Protein: 8.7g;Carbs: 13g.

Mediterranean Grilled Sea Bass

Servings:6

Cooking Time: 20 Minutes

Ingredients:

- ¼ teaspoon onion powder
- ¼ teaspoon garlic powder
- ¼ teaspoon paprika
- Lemon pepper and sea salt to taste
- 2 pounds sea bass
- 3 tablespoons extra-virgin olive oil, divided
- 2 large cloves garlic, chopped
- 1 tablespoon chopped Italian flat leaf parsley

Directions:

1. Preheat the grill to high heat.

2. Place the onion powder, garlic powder, paprika, lemon pepper, and sea salt in a large bowl and stir to combine.

3. Dredge the fish in the spice mixture, turning until well coated.

4. Heat 2 tablespoon of olive oil in a small skillet. Add the garlic and parsley and cook for 1 to 2 minutes, stirring occasionally. Remove the skillet from the heat and set aside.

5. Brush the grill grates lightly with remaining 1 tablespoon olive oil.

6. Grill the fish for about 7 minutes. Flip the fish and drizzle with the garlic mixture and cook for an additional 7 minutes, or until the fish flakes when pressed lightly with a fork.

7. Serve hot.

Nutrition:

- Info Per Serving: Calories: 200;Fat: 10.3g;Protein: 26.9g;Carbs: 0.6g.

Herby Cod Skewers

Servings:4

Cooking Time:30 Minutes

Ingredients:

- 1 lb cod fillets, cut into chunks
- 2 sweet peppers, cut into chunks
- 2 tbsp olive oil
- 2 oranges, juiced
- 1 tbsp Dijon mustard
- 1 tsp dried dill
- 1 tsp dried parsley
- Salt and black pepper to taste

Directions:

1. Mix olive oil, orange juice, dill, parsley, mustard, salt, and pepper in a bowl. Stir in cod to coat. Allow sitting for 10 minutes. Heat the grill over medium heat. Thread the cod and peppers onto skewers. Grill for 7-8 minutes, turning regularly until the fish is cooked through.

Nutrition:

- Info Per Serving: Calories: 244;Fat: 8g;Protein: 27g;Carbs: 15.5g.

Caper & Squid Stew

Servings:4
Cooking Time:25 Minutes
Ingredients:

- 2 tbsp olive oil
- 1 onion, chopped
- 1 celery stalk, chopped
- 1 lb calamari rings
- 2 red chili peppers, chopped
- 2 garlic cloves, minced
- 14 oz canned tomatoes, diced
- 2 tbsp tomato paste
- Salt and black pepper to taste
- 2 tbsp capers, drained
- 12 black olives, pitted and halved

Directions:

1. Warm the olive oil in a skillet over medium heat and cook onion, celery, garlic, and chili peppers for 2 minutes. Stir in calamari rings, tomatoes, tomato paste, salt, and pepper and bring to a simmer. Cook for 20 minutes. Put in olives and capers and cook for another 5 minutes. Serve right away.

Nutrition:

- Info Per Serving: Calories: 280;Fat: 12g;Protein: 16g;Carbs: 14g.

Walnut-crusted Salmon

Servings:4
Cooking Time:25 Minutes
Ingredients:

- 2 tbsp olive oil
- 4 salmon fillets, boneless
- 2 tbsp mustard
- 5 tsp honey
- 1 cup walnuts, chopped
- 1 tbsp lemon juice
- 2 tsp parsley, chopped
- Salt and pepper to the taste

Directions:

1. Preheat the oven to 380F. Line a baking tray with parchment paper. In a bowl, whisk the olive oil, mustard, and honey. In a separate bowl, combine walnuts and parsley. Sprinkle salmon with salt and pepper and place them on the tray. Rub each fillet with mustard mixture and scatter with walnut mixture; bake for 15 minutes. Drizzle with lemon juice.

Nutrition:

- Info Per Serving: Calories: 300;Fat: 16g;Protein: 17g;Carbs: 22g.

Lemon Rosemary Roasted Branzino

Servings:2
Cooking Time: 30 Minutes
Ingredients:

- 4 tablespoons extra-virgin olive oil, divided
- 2 branzino fillets, preferably at least 1 inch thick
- 1 garlic clove, minced
- 1 bunch scallions (white part only), thinly sliced
- 10 to 12 small cherry tomatoes, halved
- 1 large carrot, cut into ¼-inch rounds
- ½ cup dry white wine
- 2 tablespoons paprika
- 2 teaspoons kosher salt
- ½ tablespoon ground chili pepper
- 2 rosemary sprigs or 1 tablespoon dried rosemary
- 1 small lemon, thinly sliced
- ½ cup sliced pitted kalamata olives

Directions:

1. Heat a large ovenproof skillet over high heat unt hot, about 2 minutes. Add 1 tablespoon of olive oil an heat for 10 to 15 seconds until it shimmers.

2. Add the branzino fillets, skin-side up, and sear fc 2 minutes. Flip the fillets and cook for an additional minutes. Set aside.

3. Swirl 2 tablespoons of olive oil around the skillet t coat evenly.

4. Add the garlic, scallions, tomatoes, and carrot, an sauté for 5 minutes, or until softened.

5. Add the wine, stirring until all ingredients are we combined. Carefully place the fish over the sauce.

6. Preheat the oven to 450°F.

7. Brush the fillets with the remaining 1 tablespoon olive oil and season with paprika, salt, and chili peppe Top each fillet with a rosemary sprig and lemon slice Scatter the olives over fish and around the skillet.

8. Roast for about 10 minutes until the lemon slic are browned. Serve hot.

Nutrition:

- Info Per Serving: Calories: 724;Fat: 43.0g;Protei 57.7g;Carbs: 25.0g.

Thyme Hake With Potatoes

Servings:4
Cooking Time:40 Minutes
Ingredients:

1 ½ lb russet potatoes, unpeeled

¼ cup olive oil

½ tsp garlic powder

½ tsp paprika

Salt and black pepper to taste

4 skinless hake fillets

4 fresh thyme sprigs

1 lemon, sliced

Directions:

Preheat oven to 425 F. Slice the potatoes and toss them with some olive oil, salt, pepper, paprika, and garlic powder in a bowl. Microwave for 12-14 minutes until potatoes are just tender, stirring halfway through microwaving.

Transfer the potatoes to a baking dish and press gently into an even layer. Season the hake with salt and pepper, and arrange it skinned side down over the potatoes. Drizzle with the remaining olive oil, then place thyme sprigs and lemon slices on top. Bake for -18 minutes until hake flakes apart when gently prodded with a paring knife. Serve and enjoy!

Nutrition:

Info Per Serving: Calories: 410;Fat: 16g;Protein: g;Carbs: 33g.

Asian-inspired Tuna Lettuce Wraps

Servings:2
Cooking Time: 0 Minutes
Ingredients:

⅓ cup almond butter

1 tablespoon freshly squeezed lemon juice

1 teaspoon low-sodium soy sauce

1 teaspoon curry powder

½ teaspoon sriracha, or to taste

½ cup canned water chestnuts, drained and chopped

2 package tuna packed in water, drained

2 large butter lettuce leaves

Directions:

Stir together the almond butter, lemon juice, soy sauce, curry powder, sriracha in a medium bowl until well mixed. Add the water chestnuts and tuna and stir until well incorporated.

2. Place 2 butter lettuce leaves on a flat work surface, spoon half of the tuna mixture onto each leaf and roll up into a wrap. Serve immediately.

Nutrition:

• Info Per Serving: Calories: 270;Fat: 13.9g;Protein: 19.1g;Carbs: 18.5g.

Halibut Confit With Sautéed Leeks

Servings:4
Cooking Time:45 Minutes
Ingredients:

• 1 tsp fresh lemon zest

• ¼ cup olive oil

• 4 skinless halibut fillets

• Salt and black pepper to taste

• 1 lb leeks, sliced

• 1 tsp Dijon mustard

• ¾ cup dry white wine

• 1 tbsp fresh cilantro, chopped

• 4 lemon wedges

Directions:

1. Warm the olive oil in a skillet over medium heat. Season the halibut with salt and pepper. Sear in the skillet for 6-7 minutes until cooked all the way through. Carefully transfer the halibut to a large plate. Add leeks, mustard, salt, and pepper to the skillet and sauté for 10-12 minutes, stirring frequently, until softened. Pour in the wine and lemon zest and bring to a simmer. Top with halibut. Reduce the heat to low, cover, and simmer for 6-10 minutes. Carefully transfer halibut to a serving platter, tent loosely with aluminum foil, and let rest while finishing leeks. Increase the heat and cook the leeks for 2-4 minutes until the sauce is slightly thickened. Adjust the seasoning with salt and pepper. Pour the leek mixture around the halibut, sprinkle with cilantro, and serve with lemon wedges.

Nutrition:

• Info Per Serving: Calories: 566;Fat: 19g;Protein: 78g;Carbs: 17g.

Bell Pepper & Scallop Skillet

Servings:4
Cooking Time:25 Minutes
Ingredients:

- 3 tbsp olive oil
- 2 celery stalks, sliced
- 2 lb sea scallops, halved
- 3 garlic cloves, minced
- Juice of 1 lime
- 1 red bell pepper, chopped
- 1 tbsp capers, chopped
- 1 tbsp mayonnaise
- 1 tbsp rosemary, chopped
- 1 cup chicken stock

Directions:

1. Warm olive oil in a skillet over medium heat and cook celery and garlic for 2 minutes. Stir in bell pepper, lime juice, capers, rosemary, and stock and bring to a boil. Simmer for 8 minutes. Mix in scallops and mayonnaise and cook for 5 minutes.

Nutrition:

- Info Per Serving: Calories: 310;Fat: 16g;Protein: 9g;Carbs: 33g.

Mediterranean Braised Cod With Vegetables

Servings:2
Cooking Time: 18 Minutes
Ingredients:

- 1 tablespoon olive oil
- ½ medium onion, minced
- 2 garlic cloves, minced
- 1 teaspoon oregano
- 1 can artichoke hearts in water, drained and halved
- 1 can diced tomatoes with basil
- ¼ cup pitted Greek olives, drained
- 10 ounces wild cod
- Salt and freshly ground black pepper, to taste

Directions:

1. In a skillet, heat the olive oil over medium-high heat.

2. Sauté the onion for about 5 minutes, stirring occasionally, or until tender.

3. Stir in the garlic and oregano and cook for 30 seconds more until fragrant.

4. Add the artichoke hearts, tomatoes, and olives and stir to combine. Top with the cod.

5. Cover and cook for 10 minutes, or until the fi flakes easily with a fork and juices run clean.

6. Sprinkle with the salt and pepper. Serve warm.

Nutrition:

- Info Per Serving: Calories: 332;Fat: 10.5g;Prote 29.2g;Carbs: 30.7g.

Roasted Red Snapper With Citru Topping

Servings:2
Cooking Time:35 Minutes
Ingredients:

- 2 tbsp olive oil
- 1 tsp fresh cilantro, chopped
- ½ tsp grated lemon zest
- ½ tbsp lemon juice
- ½ tsp grated grapefruit zest
- ½ tbsp grapefruit juice
- ½ tsp grated orange zest
- ½ tbsp orange juice
- ½ shallot, minced
- ¼ tsp red pepper flakes
- Salt and black pepper to taste
- 1 whole red snapper, cleaned

Directions:

1. Preheat oven to 380F. Whisk the olive oil, cilant lemon juice, orange juice, grapefruit juice, shallot, a pepper flakes together in a bowl. Season with salt a pepper. Set aside the citrus topping until ready to ser

2. In a separate bowl, combine lemon zest, oran zest, grapefruit zest, salt, and pepper. With a sh knife, make 3-4 shallow slashes, about 2 inches apa on both sides of the snapper. Spoon the citrus mixtu into the fish cavity and transfer to a greased baki sheet. Roast for 25 minutes until the fish flakes. Se drizzled with citrus topping, and enjoy!

Nutrition:

- Info Per Serving: Calories: 257;Fat: 21g;Prote 16g;Carbs: 1.6g.

Moules Mariniere (mussels In Wine Sauce)

Servings:4
Cooking Time:15 Minutes
Ingredients:

- 4 tbsp butter
- 4 lb cleaned mussels
- 2 cups dry white wine
- ½ tsp sea salt
- 6 garlic cloves, minced
- 1 shallot, diced
- ½ cup chopped parsley
- Juice of ½ lemon

Directions:

1. Pour the white wine, salt, garlic, shallots, and ¼ cup of the parsley into a large saucepan over medium heat. Cover and bring to boil. Add the mussels and simmer just until all of the mussels open, about 6 minutes. Do not overcook. With a slotted spoon, remove the mussels to a bowl. Add the butter and lemon juice to the saucepan, stir, and pour the broth over the mussels. Garnish with the remaining parsley and serve with a crusty, wholegrain baguette.

Nutrition:

Info Per Serving: Calories: 528;Fat: 24g;Protein: 55g;Carbs: 20g.

Seared Halibut With Moroccan Chermoula

Servings:4
Cooking Time:30 Min + Marinating Time
Ingredients:

- 2 tbsp olive oil
- 1 tsp dry thyme
- 1 tsp dry rosemary
- 4 halibut steaks
- Salt and black pepper to taste
- Chermoula
- 2 tbsp olive oil
- ¾ cup fresh cilantro
- 2 tbsp lemon juice
- 4 garlic cloves, minced
- ½ tsp ground cumin
- ½ tsp paprika
- ¼ tsp salt
- ½ tsp cayenne pepper

Directions:

1. In a large bowl, coat the fish with 2 tbsp olive oil, rosemary, thyme, salt, and pepper. Let it marinate for 15 minutes. Process cilantro, lemon juice, olive oil, garlic, cumin, paprika, salt, and cayenne pepper in your food processor until smooth, about 1 minute, scraping down sides of the bowl as needed. Set aside the chermoula until ready to serve.

2. Preheat oven to 325 F. Place the halibut in a baking tray. Bake for 10-12 minutes until halibut flakes apart when gently prodded with a paring knife. Serve with chermoula.

Nutrition:

- Info Per Serving: Calories: 187;Fat: 11g;Protein: 19g;Carbs: 1.1g.

Hake Fillet In Herby Tomato Sauce

Servings:4
Cooking Time:30 Minutes
Ingredients:

- 2 tbsp olive oil
- 1 onion, sliced thin
- 1 fennel bulb, sliced
- Salt and black pepper to taste
- 4 garlic cloves, minced
- 1 tsp fresh thyme, chopped
- 1 can diced tomatoes,
- ½ cup dry white wine
- 4 skinless hake fillets
- 2 tbsp fresh basil, chopped

Directions:

1. Warm the olive oil in a skillet over medium heat. Sauté the onion and fennel for about 5 minutes until softened. Stir in garlic and thyme and cook for about 30 seconds until fragrant. Pour in tomatoes and wine and bring to simmer.

2. Season the hake with salt and pepper. Nestle hake skinned side down into the tomato sauce and spoon some sauce over the top. Bring to simmer. Cook for 10-12 minutes until hake easily flakes with a fork. Sprinkle with basil and serve.

Nutrition:

- Info Per Serving: Calories: 452;Fat: 9.9g;Protein: 78g;Carbs: 9.7g.

Lemon-parsley Swordfish

Servings:4
Cooking Time: 17 To 20 Minutes
Ingredients:
- 1 cup fresh Italian parsley
- ¼ cup lemon juice
- ¼ cup extra-virgin olive oil
- ¼ cup fresh thyme
- 2 cloves garlic
- ½ teaspoon salt
- 4 swordfish steaks
- Olive oil spray

Directions:
1. Preheat the oven to 450°F. Grease a large baking dish generously with olive oil spray.
2. Place the parsley, lemon juice, olive oil, thyme, garlic, and salt in a food processor and pulse until smoothly blended.
3. Arrange the swordfish steaks in the greased baking dish and spoon the parsley mixture over the top.
4. Bake in the preheated oven for 17 to 20 minutes until flaky.
5. Divide the fish among four plates and serve hot.
Nutrition:
- Info Per Serving: Calories: 396;Fat: 21.7g;Protein: 44.2g;Carbs: 2.9g.

Hot Jumbo Shrimp

Servings:4
Cooking Time:20 Minutes
Ingredients:
- 2 lb shell-on jumbo shrimp, deveined
- ¼ cup olive oil
- Salt and black pepper to taste
- 6 garlic cloves, minced
- 1 tsp anise seeds
- ½ tsp red pepper flakes
- 2 tbsp minced fresh cilantro
- 1 lemon, cut into wedges

Directions:
1. Combine the olive oil, garlic, anise seeds, pepper flakes, and black pepper in a large bowl. Add the shrimp and cilantro and toss well, making sure the oil mixture gets into the interior of the shrimp. Arrange shrimp in a single layer on a baking tray. Set under the preheated broiler for approximately 4 minutes. Flip shrimp and continue to broil until it is opaque and shells are beginning to brown, about 2 minutes, rotating sheet halfway through broiling. Serve with lemon wedges.
Nutrition:

- Info Per Serving: Calories: 218;Fat: 9g;Protein 30.8g;Carbs: 2.3g.

Calamari In Garlic-cilantro Sauce

Servings:4
Cooking Time:25 Minutes
Ingredients:
- 2 tbsp olive oil
- 2 lb calamari, sliced into rings
- 4 garlic cloves, minced
- 1 lime, juiced
- 2 tbsp balsamic vinegar
- 3 tbsp cilantro, chopped

Directions:
1. Warm the olive oil in a skillet over medium hea and sauté garlic, lime juice, balsamic vinegar, an cilantro for 5 minutes. Stir in calamari rings and coo for 10 minutes.
Nutrition:
- Info Per Serving: Calories: 290;Fat: 19g;Protei 19g;Carbs: 10g.

Herby Mackerel Fillets In Red Sauce

Servings:2
Cooking Time:15 Minutes
Ingredients:
- 1 tbsp butter
- 2 mackerel fillets
- ¼ cup white wine
- ½ cup spring onions, sliced
- 2 garlic cloves, minced
- ½ tsp dried thyme
- 1 tsp dried parsley
- Salt and black pepper to taste
- ½ cup vegetable broth
- ½ cup tomato sauce
- ½ tsp hot sauce
- 1 tbsp fresh mint, chopped

Directions:
1. In a pot over medium heat, melt the butter. Add fish and cook for 6 minutes in total; set aside. Pour the wine and scrape off any bits from the bottom. Ac in spring onions and garlic; cook for 3 minutes unt fragrant. Sprinkle with thyme, parsley, salt, and peppe Stir in vegetable broth, tomato sauce, and add back th fillets. Cook for 3-4 minutes. Stir in hot sauce and tc with mint. Serve and enjoy!
Nutrition:
- Info Per Serving: Calories: 334;Fat: 22g;Protei 23.8g;Carbs: 7g.

Instant Pot Poached Salmon

Servings:4

Cooking Time: 3 Minutes

Ingredients:

1 lemon, sliced ¼ inch thick

4 skinless salmon fillets, 1½ inches thick

½ teaspoon salt

¼ teaspoon pepper

½ cup water

Directions:

Layer the lemon slices in the bottom of the Instant Pot.

Season the salmon with salt and pepper, then arrange the salmon (skin- side down) on top of the lemon slices. Pour in the water.

Secure the lid. Select the Manual mode and set the cooking time for 3 minutes at High Pressure.

Once cooking is complete, do a quick pressure release. Carefully open the lid.

Serve warm.

Nutrition:

Info Per Serving: Calories: 350;Fat: 23.0g;Protein: 5.0g;Carbs: 0g.

Lime-orange Squid Meal

Servings:4

Cooking Time:30 Minutes

Ingredients:

1 lb baby squid, cleaned, body and tentacles chopped

3 tbsp olive oil

½ cup green olives, chopped

½ tsp lime zest, grated

1 tbsp lime juice

½ tsp orange zest, grated

1 tsp red pepper flakes

1 tbsp parsley, chopped

4 garlic cloves, minced

1 shallot, chopped

1 cup vegetable stock

2 tbsp red wine vinegar

Salt and black pepper to taste

Directions:

Warm the olive oil in a skillet over medium heat and stir in lime zest, lime juice, orange zest, red pepper flakes, garlic, shallot, olives, stock, vinegar, salt, and pepper. Bring to a boil and simmer for 10 minutes. Mix

in squid and parsley and cook for another 10 minutes. Serve hot.

Nutrition:

- Info Per Serving: Calories: 310;Fat: 10g;Protein: 12g;Carbs: 23g.

Lemony Shrimp With Orzo Salad

Servings:4

Cooking Time: 22 Minutes

Ingredients:

- 1 cup orzo
- 1 hothouse cucumber, deseeded and chopped
- ½ cup finely diced red onion
- 2 tablespoons extra-virgin olive oil
- 2 pounds shrimp, peeled and deveined
- 3 lemons, juiced
- Salt and freshly ground black pepper, to taste
- ¾ cup crumbled feta cheese
- 2 tablespoons dried dill
- 1 cup chopped fresh flat-leaf parsley

Directions:

1. Bring a large pot of water to a boil. Add the orzo and cook covered for 15 to 18 minutes, or until the orzo is tender. Transfer to a colander to drain and set aside to cool.

2. Mix the cucumber and red onion in a bowl. Set aside.

3. Heat the olive oil in a medium skillet over medium heat until it shimmers.

4. Reduce the heat, add the shrimp, and cook each side for 2 minutes until cooked through.

5. Add the cooked shrimp to the bowl of cucumber and red onion. Mix in the cooked orzo and lemon juice and toss to combine. Sprinkle with salt and pepper. Scatter the top with the feta cheese and dill. Garnish with the parsley and serve immediately.

Nutrition:

- Info Per Serving: Calories: 565;Fat: 17.8g;Protein: 63.3g;Carbs: 43.9g.

Spiced Flounder With Pasta Salad

Servings:4
Cooking Time:25 Minutes
Ingredients:

- 2 tbsp olive oil
- 4 flounder fillets, boneless
- 1 tsp rosemary, dried
- 2 tsp cumin, ground
- 1 tbsp coriander, ground
- 2 tsp cinnamon powder
- 2 tsp oregano, dried
- Salt and black pepper to taste
- 2 cups macaroni, cooked
- 1 cup cherry tomatoes, halved
- 1 avocado, peeled and sliced
- 1 cucumber, cubed
- ½ cup black olives, sliced
- 1 lemon, juiced

Directions:

1. Preheat the oven to 390 F. Combine rosemary, cumin, coriander, cinnamon, oregano, salt, and pepper in a bowl. Add in the flounder and toss to coat.
2. Warm olive oil in a skillet over medium heat. Brown the fish fillets for 4 minutes on both sides. Transfer to a baking tray and bake in the oven for 7-10 minutes. Combine macaroni, tomatoes, avocado, cucumber, olives, and lemon juice in a bowl; toss to coat. Serve the fish with pasta salad on the side.

Nutrition:

- Info Per Serving: Calories: 370;Fat: 16g;Protein: 26g;Carbs: 57g.

Seafood Cakes With Radicchio Salad

Servings:4
Cooking Time:30 Minutes
Ingredients:

- 2 tbsp butter
- 2 tbsp extra-virgin olive oil
- 1 lb lump crabmeat
- 4 scallions, sliced
- 1 garlic clove, minced
- ¼ cup cooked shrimp
- 2 tbsp heavy cream
- ¼ head radicchio, thinly sliced

- 1 green apple, shredded
- 2 tbsp lemon juice
- Salt and black pepper to taste

Directions:

1. In a food processor, place the shrimp, heavy crea[m], salt, and pepper. Blend until smooth. Mix crab me[at] and scallions in a bowl. Add in shrimp mixture a[nd] toss to combine. Make 4 patties out of the mixtu[re.] Transfer to the fridge for 10 minutes. Warm butter i[n a] skillet over medium heat and brown patties for [] minutes on all sides. Remove to a serving plate. M[ix] radicchio and apple in a bowl. Combine olive oil, lem[on] juice, garlic, and salt in a small bowl and stir well. Po[ur] over the salad and toss to combine. Serve and enjoy!

Nutrition:

- Info Per Serving: Calories: 238;Fat: 14.3g;Prote[in:] 20g;Carbs: 8g.

Mackerel And Green Bean Salad

Servings:2
Cooking Time: 10 Minutes
Ingredients:

- 2 cups green beans
- 1 tablespoon avocado oil
- 2 mackerel fillets
- 4 cups mixed salad greens
- 2 hard-boiled eggs, sliced
- 1 avocado, sliced
- 2 tablespoons lemon juice
- 2 tablespoons olive oil
- 1 teaspoon Dijon mustard
- Salt and black pepper, to taste

Directions:

1. Cook the green beans in a medium saucepan [of] boiling water for about 3 minutes until crisp-tend[er]. Drain and set aside.
2. Melt the avocado oil in a pan over medium he[at]. Add the mackerel fillets and cook each side for [] minutes.
3. Divide the greens between two salad bowls. T[op] with the mackerel, sliced egg, and avocado slices.
4. In another bowl, whisk together the lemon jui[ce,] olive oil, mustard, salt, and pepper, and drizzle o[ver] the salad. Add the cooked green beans and toss [to] combine, then serve.

Nutrition:

- Info Per Serving: Calories: 737;Fat: 57.3g;Prote[in:] 34.2g;Carbs: 22.1g.

Poultry And Meats Recipes

Beef With Zucchini & Mozzarella

Servings:4
Cooking Time:40 Minutes
Ingredients:

- 15 oz canned roasted tomatoes, crushed
- 1 tbsp olive oil
- 1 lb beef meat, cubed
- ¾ cup mozzarella, shredded
- 2 zucchinis, chopped
- 1 onion, chopped
- 2 garlic cloves, minced
- 1 tsp dried oregano
- Salt and black pepper to taste

Directions:

1. Warm the olive oil in a skillet over medium heat and sear beef for 5 minutes. Stir in zucchinis, onion, garlic, oregano, salt, pepper, and tomatoes and bring to a boil. Simmer for 20 minutes. Mix in mozzarella cheese and stir for 2-3 minutes.

Nutrition:

Info Per Serving: Calories: 318;Fat: 17g;Protein: 9g;Carbs: 16g.

Tzatziki Chicken Loaf

Servings:4
Cooking Time:70 Min + Chilling Time
Ingredients:

- 1 lb ground chicken
- 1 onion, chopped
- 1 tsp garlic powder
- 1 cup tzatziki sauce
- ½ tsp dried Greek oregano
- ½ tsp dried cilantro
- ½ tsp sweet paprika
- Salt and black pepper to taste

Directions:

1. Preheat oven to 350 F. In a bowl, add chicken, paprika, onion, Greek oregano, cilantro, garlic, salt, and pepper and mix well with your hands. Shape the mixture into a greased loaf pan and bake in the oven for 55-60 minutes. Let sit for 15 minutes and slice. Serve topped with tzatziki sauce.

Nutrition:

Info Per Serving: Calories: 240;Fat: 9g;Protein: 3.2g;Carbs: 3.6g.

Vegetable & Turkey Traybake

Servings:4
Cooking Time:80 Minutes
Ingredients:

- 2 tbsp olive oil
- 1 lb turkey breast, cubed
- 1 head broccoli, cut into florets
- 2 oz cherry tomatoes, halved
- 2 tbsp cilantro, chopped
- 1 lemon, zested
- Salt and black pepper to taste
- 2 spring onions, chopped

Directions:

1. Preheat the oven to 360 F. Warm the olive oil in a skillet over medium heat and sauté spring onions and lemon zest for 3 minutes. Add in turkey and cook for another 5-6 minutes, stirring occasionally. Transfer to a baking dish, pour in 1 cup of water and bake for 30 minutes. Add in broccoli and tomatoes and bake for another 10 minutes. Top with cilantro.

Nutrition:

- Info Per Serving: Calories: 310;Fat: 10g;Protein: 15g;Carbs: 21g.

Pork Millet With Chestnuts

Servings:6
Cooking Time:30 Minutes
Ingredients:

- 2 cups pork roast, cooked and shredded
- ½ cup sour cream
- 1 cup millet
- 3 oz water chestnuts, sliced
- Salt and white pepper to taste

Directions:

1. Place millet and salted water in a pot over medium heat and cook for 20 minutes. Drain and remove to a bowl to cool. When ready, add in pork, chestnuts, cream, salt, and pepper and mix to combine. Serve.

Nutrition:

- Info Per Serving: Calories: 300;Fat: 18g;Protein: 24g;Carbs: 17g.

Chicken Pappardelle With Mushrooms

Servings:2
Cooking Time:30 Minutes
Ingredients:
- 4 oz cremini mushrooms, sliced
- 2 tbsp olive oil
- ½ onion, minced
- 2 garlic cloves, minced
- 8 oz chicken breasts, cubed
- 2 tsp tomato paste
- 2 tsp dried tarragon
- 2 cups chicken stock
- 6 oz pappardelle pasta
- ¼ cup Greek yogurt
- Salt and black pepper to taste
- ¼ tsp red pepper flakes

Directions:
1. Warm 1 tablespoon of olive oil in a pan over medium heat. Suté the onion, garlic, and mushrooms for 5 minutes. Move the vegetables to the edges of the pan and add the remaining 1 tablespoon of olive oil to the center of the pan. Place the chicken cubes in the center and let them cook for about 6 minutes, stirring often until golden brown.

2. Mix in the tomato paste and tarragon. Add the chicken stock and stir well to combine everything. Bring the mixture to a boil. Add the pappardelle. Simmer covered for 9-11 minutes, stirring occasionally, until the pasta is cooked and the liquid is mostly absorbed. Remove the pan from the heat. Stir 2 tbsp of the hot liquid from the pan into the yogurt. Pour the tempered yogurt into the pan and stir well to mix it into the sauce. Season with salt and pepper. Top with pepper flakes.

Nutrition:
- Info Per Serving: Calories: 556;Fat: 18g;Protein: 42g;Carbs: 56g.

Pork Chops In Wine Sauce

Servings:4
Cooking Time:30 Minutes
Ingredients:
- 2 tbsp olive oil
- 4 pork chops
- 1 cup red onion, sliced
- 10 black peppercorns, crushed
- ¼ cup vegetable stock
- ¼ cup dry white wine
- 2 garlic cloves, minced
- Salt to taste

Directions:
1. Warm the olive oil in a skillet over medium hea and sear pork chops for 8 minutes on both sides. Put i onion and garlic and cook for another 2 minutes. M in stock, wine, salt, and peppercorns and cook for 1 minutes, stirring often.

Nutrition:
- Info Per Serving: Calories: 240;Fat: 10g;Protei 25g;Carbs: 14g.

Cocktail Meatballs In Almond Sauce

Servings:4
Cooking Time:30 Minutes
Ingredients:
- 3 tbsp olive oil
- 8 oz ground pork
- 8 oz ground beef
- ½ cup finely minced onions
- 1 large egg, beaten
- 1 potato, shredded
- Salt and black pepper to taste
- 1 tsp garlic powder
- ½ tsp oregano
- 2 tbsp chopped parsley
- ¼ cup ground almonds
- 1 cup chicken broth
- ¼ cup butter

Directions:
1. Place the ground meat, onions, egg, potato, sa garlic powder, pepper, and oregano in a large bow Shape the mixture into small meatballs, about 1 inch diameter, and place on a plate. Let sit for 10 minutes room temperature.

2. Warm the olive oil in a skillet over medium hea Add the meatballs and brown them for 6-8 minutes all sides; reserve. In the hot skillet, melt the butter ar add the almonds and broth. Cook for 3-5 minutes. Ad the meatballs to the skillet, cover, and cook for 8-1 minutes. Top with parsley.

Nutrition:
- Info Per Serving: Calories: 449;Fat: 42g;Protei 16g;Carbs: 3g.

Greek Beef Kebabs

Servings:2
Cooking Time: 20 Minutes
Ingredients:

6 ounces beef sirloin tip, trimmed of fat and cut to 2-inch pieces

3 cups of any mixture of vegetables: mushrooms, summer squash, zucchini, onions, red peppers, cherry tomatoes

½ cup olive oil

¼ cup freshly squeezed lemon juice

2 tablespoons balsamic vinegar

2 teaspoons dried oregano

1 teaspoon garlic powder

1 teaspoon salt

1 teaspoon minced fresh rosemary

Cooking spray

Directions:

Put the beef in a plastic freezer bag.

Slice the vegetables into similar-size pieces and put them in a second freezer bag.

Make the marinade: Mix the olive oil, lemon juice, balsamic vinegar, oregano, garlic powder, salt, and rosemary in a measuring cup. Whisk well to combine. Pour half of the marinade over the beef, and the other half over the vegetables.

Put the beef and vegetables in the refrigerator to marinate for 4 hours.

When ready, preheat the grill to medium-high heat and spray the grill grates with cooking spray.

Thread the meat onto skewers and the vegetables into separate skewers.

Grill the meat for 3 minutes per side. They should only take 10 to 12 minutes to cook, depending on the thickness of the meat.

Grill the vegetables for about 3 minutes per side, or until they have grill marks and are softened. Serve hot.

Nutrition:

Info Per Serving: Calories: 284;Fat: 18.2g;Protein: .0g;Carbs: 9.0g.

Cranberry Turkey Bake

Servings:4
Cooking Time:40 Minutes
Ingredients:

2 tbsp canola oil

1 turkey breast, sliced

1 cup chicken stock

- ½ cup cranberry sauce
- ½ cup orange juice
- 1 tsp mustard powder
- 1 onion, chopped
- Salt and black pepper to taste

Directions:

1. Warm canola oil in a saucepan over medium heat. Cook onion for 3 minutes. Put in turkey and cook for another 5 minutes, turning once. Season with mustard powder, salt, and pepper. Pour in the cranberry sauce, chicken stock, and orange juice and bring to a boil; simmer for 20 minutes.

Nutrition:

- Info Per Serving: Calories: 390;Fat: 14g;Protein: 19g;Carbs: 28g.

Spiced Roast Chicken

Servings:6
Cooking Time: 35 Minutes
Ingredients:

- 1 teaspoon garlic powder
- 1 teaspoon ground paprika
- ½ teaspoon ground cumin
- ½ teaspoon ground coriander
- ½ teaspoon salt
- ¼ teaspoon ground cayenne pepper
- 6 chicken legs
- 1 teaspoon extra-virgin olive oil

Directions:

1. Preheat the oven to 400°F.

2. Combine the garlic powder, paprika, cumin, coriander, salt, and cayenne pepper in a small bowl.

3. On a clean work surface, rub the spices all over the chicken legs until completely coated.

4. Heat the olive oil in an ovenproof skillet over medium heat.

5. Add the chicken thighs and sear each side for 8 to 10 minutes, or until the skin is crispy and browned.

6. Transfer the skillet to the preheated oven and continue cooking for 10 to 15 minutes, or until the juices run clear and it registers an internal temperature of 165°F.

7. Remove from the heat and serve on plates.

Nutrition:

- Info Per Serving: Calories: 275;Fat: 15.6g;Protein: 30.3g;Carbs: 0.9g.

Chicken & Spinach Dish

Servings:4
Cooking Time:60 Minutes
Ingredients:

- 2 tbsp olive oil
- 2 cups baby spinach
- 1 lb chicken sausage, sliced
- 1 red bell pepper, chopped
- 1 onion, sliced
- 2 tbsp garlic, minced
- Salt and black pepper to taste
- ½ cup chicken stock
- 1 tbsp balsamic vinegar

Directions:

1. Preheat oven to 380 F. Warm olive oil in a skillet over medium heat. Cook sausages for 6 minutes on all sides. Remove to a bowl. Add the bell pepper, onion, garlic, salt, pepper to the skillet and sauté for 5 minutes. Pour in stock and vinegar and return the sausages. Bring to a boil and cook for 10 minutes. Add in the spinach and cook until wilts, about 4 minutes. Serve and enjoy!

Nutrition:

- Info Per Serving: Calories: 300;Fat: 15g;Protein: 27g;Carbs: 18g.

Greek-style Chicken & Egg Bake

Servings:4
Cooking Time:45 Minutes
Ingredients:

- ½ lb Halloumi cheese, grated
- 1 tbsp olive oil
- 1 lb chicken breasts, cubed
- 4 eggs, beaten
- 1 tsp dry mustard
- 2 cloves garlic, crushed
- 2 red bell peppers, sliced
- 1 red onion, sliced
- 2 tomatoes, chopped
- 1 tsp sweet paprika
- ½ tsp dried basil
- Salt to taste

Directions:

1. Preheat oven to 360 F. Warm the olive oil in a skillet over medium heat. Add the bell peppers, garlic, onion, and salt and cook for 3 minutes. Stir in tomatoes for an additional 5 minutes. Put in chicken breasts, paprika, dry mustard, and basil. Cook for

another 6-8 minutes. Transfer the mixture to a greas[ed] baking pan and pour over the beaten eggs; season w[ith] salt. Bake for 15-18 minutes. Remove and spread t[he] cheese over the top. Let cool for a few minutes. Se[rve] sliced.

Nutrition:

- Info Per Serving: Calories: 480;Fat: 31g;Prote[in:] 39g;Carbs: 12g.

Beef Kebabs With Onion And Pepper

Servings:6
Cooking Time: 10 Minutes
Ingredients:

- 2 pounds beef fillet
- 1½ teaspoons salt
- 1 teaspoon freshly ground black pepper
- ½ teaspoon ground nutmeg
- ½ teaspoon ground allspice
- ⅓ cup extra-virgin olive oil
- 1 large onion, cut into 8 quarters
- 1 large red bell pepper, cut into 1-inch cubes

Directions:

1. Preheat the grill to high heat.
2. Cut the beef into 1-inch cubes and put them i[n a] large bowl.
3. In a small bowl, mix together the salt, black pep[per,] allspice, and nutmeg.
4. Pour the olive oil over the beef and toss to co[at.] Evenly sprinkle the seasoning over the beef and toss [to] coat all pieces.
5. Skewer the beef, alternating every 1 or 2 pie[ces] with a piece of onion or bell pepper.
6. To cook, place the skewers on the preheated gr[ill] and flip every 2 to 3 minutes until all sides have coo[ked] to desired doneness, 6 minutes for medium-rare, [8] minutes for well done. Serve hot.

Nutrition:

- Info Per Serving: Calories: 485;Fat: 36.0g;Prote[in:] 35.0g;Carbs: 4.0g.

Rich Beef Meal

Servings:4
Cooking Time:40 Minutes
Ingredients:

- 1 tbsp olive oil
- 1 lb beef meat, cubed
- 1 red onion, chopped
- 1 garlic clove, minced
- 1 celery stalk, chopped
- Salt and black pepper to taste
- 14 oz canned tomatoes, diced
- 1 cup vegetable stock
- ½ tsp ground nutmeg
- 2 tsp dill, chopped

Directions:

1. Warm the olive oil in a skillet over medium heat and cook onion and garlic for 5 minutes. Put in beef and cook for 5 more minutes. Stir in celery, salt, pepper, tomatoes, stock, nutmeg, and dill and bring to a boil. Cook for 20 minutes.

Nutrition:

Info Per Serving: Calories: 300;Fat: 14g;Protein: 9g;Carbs: 16g.

Curried Green Bean & Chicken Breasts

Servings:4
Cooking Time:8 Hours 10 Minutes
Ingredients:

- 12 oz green beans, chopped
- 1 lb chicken breasts, cubed
- 1 cup chicken stock
- 1 onion, chopped
- 1 tbsp white wine vinegar
- 1 cup Kalamata olives, chopped
- 1 tbsp curry powder
- 2 tsp basil, dried
- Salt and black pepper to taste

Directions:

1. Place chicken, green beans, chicken stock, onion, vinegar, olives, curry powder, basil, salt, and pepper in your slow cooker. Cover with the lid and cook for 8 hours on Low.

Nutrition:

Info Per Serving: Calories: 290;Fat: 13g;Protein: 9g;Carbs: 20g.

Slow Cooker Brussel Sprout & Chicken

Servings:4
Cooking Time:8 Hours 20 Minutes
Ingredients:

- 2 tbsp olive oil
- 1 lb Brussels sprouts, halved
- 2 lb chicken breasts, cubed
- 1 ½ cups veggie stock
- 2 red onions, sliced
- 2 garlic cloves, minced
- 1 tbsp sweet paprika
- ½ cup tomato sauce
- Salt and black pepper to taste

Directions:

1. Warm the olive oil in a skillet over medium heat and sear the chicken for 10 minutes on all sides. Remove to your slow cooker. Add in onions, stock, garlic, paprika, Brussels sprouts, tomato sauce, salt, pepper, and dill. Cover the lid and cook for 8 hours on Low. Serve immediately.

Nutrition:

- Info Per Serving: Calories: 302;Fat: 15g;Protein: 16g;Carbs: 17g.

Spinach Chicken With Chickpeas

Servings:4
Cooking Time:25 Minutes
Ingredients:

- 2 tbsp olive oil
- 1 lb chicken breasts, cubed
- 10 oz spinach, chopped
- 1 cup canned chickpeas
- 1 onion, chopped
- 2 garlic cloves, minced
- ½ cup chicken stock
- 2 tbsp Parmesan cheese, grated
- 1 tbsp parsley, chopped
- Salt and black pepper to taste

Directions:

1. Warm the olive oil in a skillet over medium heat and brown chicken for 5 minutes. Season with salt and pepper. Stir in onion and garlic for 3 minutes. Pour in stock and chickpeas and bring to a boil. Cook for 20 minutes. Mix in spinach and cook until wilted, about 5 minutes. Top with Parmesan cheese and parsley. Serve and enjoy!

Nutrition:

- Info Per Serving: Calories: 290;Fat: 10g;Protein: 35g;Carbs: 22g.

Bell Pepper & Onion Pork Chops

Servings:4
Cooking Time:30 Minutes
Ingredients:

- 2 tbsp olive oil
- 4 pork chops
- Salt and black pepper to taste
- 1 tsp fennel seeds
- 1 red bell pepper, sliced
- 1 green bell pepper, sliced
- 1 yellow onion, thinly sliced
- 2 tsp Italian seasoning
- 2 garlic cloves, minced
- 1 tbsp balsamic vinegar

Directions:

1. Warm the olive oil in a large skillet over medium heat. Season the pork chops with salt and pepper and add them to the skillet. Cook for 6-8 minutes on both sides or until golden brown; reserve. Sauté the garlic, sliced bell peppers, onions, fennel seeds, and herbs in the skillet for 6-8 minutes until tender, stirring occasionally. Return the pork, cover, and lower the heat to low. Cook for another 3 minutes or until the pork is cooked through. Transfer the pork and vegetables to a serving platter. Add the vinegar to the skillet and stir to combine for 1-2 minutes. Drizzle the sauce over the pork.

Nutrition:

- Info Per Serving: Calories: 508;Fat: 40g;Protein: 31g;Carbs: 8g.

Easy Pork Stew(1)

Servings:4
Cooking Time:50 Minutes
Ingredients:

- 1 tbsp olive oil
- 1 lb pork stew meat, cubed
- 2 shallots, chopped
- 14 oz canned tomatoes, diced
- 1 garlic clove, minced
- 3 cups beef stock
- 2 tbsp paprika
- 1 tsp coriander seeds
- 1 tsp dried thyme
- Salt and black pepper to taste
- 2 tbsp parsley, chopped

Directions:

1. Warm the olive oil in a pot over medium heat an cook pork meat for 5 minutes until brown, stirrin occasionally. Add in shallots and garlic and cook for a additional 3 minutes. Stir in beef stock, tomatoe paprika, thyme, coriander seeds, salt, and pepper an bring to a boil; cook for 30 minutes. Serve warn topped with parsley.

Nutrition:

- Info Per Serving: Calories: 330;Fat: 18g;Protein 35g;Carbs: 28g.

Spinach-cheese Stuffed Pork Loin

Servings:6
Cooking Time:55 Minutes
Ingredients:

- 1 ½ lb pork tenderloin
- 6 slices pancetta, chopped
- 1 cup mushrooms, sliced
- 5 sundried tomatoes, diced
- Salt and black pepper to taste

Directions:

1. Place a skillet over medium heat and stir-fry th pancetta for 5 minutes until crispy. Add th mushrooms and sauté for another 4-5 minutes unt tender, stirring occasionally. Stir in sundried tomatoe and season with salt and pepper; set aside. Preheat th oven to 350F. Using a sharp knife, cut the por tenderloin in half lengthwise, leaving about 1-inc border; be careful not to cut through to the other sid Open the tenderloin like a book to form a larg rectangle.

2. Flatten it to about ¼-inch thickness with a mea tenderizer. Season the pork generously with salt an pepper. Top all over with pancetta filling. Roll up por tenderloin and tightly secure with kitchen twine. Plac on a greased baking sheet. Bake for 60-75 minut until the pork is cooked through, depending on th thickness of the pork. Remove from the oven and l rest for 10 minutes at room temperature. Remove th twine and discard. Slice the pork into medallions ar serve.

Nutrition:

- Info Per Serving: Calories: 270;Fat: 21g;Protein 20g;Carbs: 2g.

Herby Turkey Stew

Servings:4
Cooking Time:60 Minutes
Ingredients:

1 skinless, boneless turkey breast, cubed

2 tbsp olive oil

Salt and black pepper to taste

1 tbsp sweet paprika

½ cup chicken stock

1 lb pearl onions

2 garlic cloves, minced

1 carrot, sliced

1 tsp cumin, ground

1 tbsp basil, chopped

1 tbsp cilantro, chopped

Directions:

Warm the olive oil in a pot over medium heat and sear turkey for 8 minutes, stirring occasionally. Stir in pearl onions, carrot, and garlic and cook for another 3 minutes. Season with salt, pepper, cumin, and paprika. Pour in the stock and bring to a boil; cook for 40 minutes. Top with basil and cilantro.

Nutrition:

Info Per Serving: Calories: 260;Fat: 12g;Protein: g;Carbs: 24g.

Provençal Flank Steak Au Pistou

Servings:4
Cooking Time:25 Minutes
Ingredients:

8 tbsp olive oil

1 lb flank steak

Salt and black pepper to taste

½ cup parsley, chopped

¼ cup fresh basil, chopped

2 garlic cloves, minced

½ tsp celery seeds

1 orange, zested and juiced

1 tsp red pepper flakes

1 tbsp red wine vinegar

Directions:

Place the parsley, basil, garlic, orange zest and juice, celery seeds, salt, pepper, and red pepper flakes, and pulse until finely chopped in your food processor. With the processor running, stream in the red wine vinegar and 6 tbsp of olive oil until well combined. Set aside until ready to serve.

2. Preheat your grill. Rub the steak with the remaining olive oil, salt, and pepper. Place the steak on the grill and cook for 6-8 minutes on each side. Remove and leave to sit for 10 minutes. Slice the steak and drizzle with pistou. Serve.

Nutrition:

• Info Per Serving: Calories: 441;Fat: 36g;Protein: 25g;Carbs: 3g.

Greek-style Chicken With Potatoes

Servings:4
Cooking Time:30 Minutes
Ingredients:

• 4 potatoes, peeled and quartered

• 4 boneless skinless chicken drumsticks

• 4 cups water

• 2 lemons, zested and juiced

• 1 tbsp olive oil

• 2 tsp fresh oregano

• Salt and black pepper to taste

• 2 Serrano peppers, minced

• 3 tbsp finely chopped parsley

• 1 cup packed watercress

• 1 cucumber, thinly chopped

• 10 cherry tomatoes, quartered

• 16 Kalamata olives, pitted

• ¼ cup hummus

• ¼ cup feta cheese, crumbled

• Lemon wedges, for serving

Directions:

1. Add water and potatoes to your Instant Pot. Set trivet over them. In a baking bowl, mix lemon juice, olive oil, black pepper, oregano, zest, salt, and Serrano peppers. Add chicken drumsticks in the marinade and stir to coat.

2. Set the bowl with chicken on the trivet in the cooker. Seal the lid, select Manual and cook on High for 15 minutes. Do a quick release. Take out the bowl with chicken and the trivet from the pot. Drain potatoes and add parsley and salt. Split the potatoes among serving plates and top with watercress, cucumber slices, hummus, cherry tomatoes, chicken, olives, and feta cheese. Garnish with lemon wedges. Serve.

Nutrition:

• Info Per Serving: Calories: 726;Fat: 15g;Protein: 72g;Carbs: 75g.

Baked Root Veggie & Chicken

Servings:6
Cooking Time:50 Minutes
Ingredients:

- 2 sweet potatoes, peeled and cubed
- ½ cup green olives, pitted and smashed
- ¼ cup olive oil
- 2 lb chicken breasts, sliced
- 2 tbsp harissa seasoning
- 1 lemon, zested and juiced
- Salt and black pepper to taste
- 2 carrots, chopped
- 1 onion, chopped
- ½ cup feta cheese, crumbled
- ½ cup parsley, chopped

Directions:

1. Preheat the oven to 390 F. Place chicken, harissa seasoning, lemon juice, lemon zest, olive oil, salt, pepper, carrots, sweet potatoes, and onion in a roasting pan and mix well. Bake for 40 minutes. Combine feta cheese and green olives in a bowl. Share chicken mixture into plates and top with olive mixture. Top with parsley and parsley and serve immediately.

Nutrition:

- Info Per Serving: Calories: 310;Fat: 10g;Protein: 15g;Carbs: 23g.

Citrusy Leg Lamb

Servings:4
Cooking Time:7 Hours 10 Minutes
Ingredients:

- 2 cups stewed tomatoes, drained
- 3 ½ lb leg of lamb, cubed
- 1 lb small potatoes, cubed
- 1 grapefruit, zested and juiced
- 4 garlic cloves, minced
- Salt and black pepper to taste
- ½ cup basil, chopped

Directions:

1. Place potatoes, tomatoes, grapefruit juice, grapefruit zest, garlic, leg of lamb, salt, and pepper in your slow cooker. Cover with lid and cook for 8 hours on Low. Top with basil.

Nutrition:

- Info Per Serving: Calories: 300;Fat: 10g;Protein: 19g;Carbs: 16g.

Tomato Caper & Turkey Pot

Servings:4
Cooking Time:8 Hours 10 Minutes
Ingredients:

- 2 tbsp capers, drained
- 1 lb turkey breast, sliced
- 2 cups canned tomatoes, diced
- 2 garlic cloves, minced
- 1 yellow onion, chopped
- 2 cups chicken stock
- ¼ cup rosemary, chopped
- Salt and black pepper to taste

Directions:

1. Place turkey, tomatoes, garlic, onion, chicken stoc capers, rosemary, salt, and pepper in your slow cook Cover with the lid and cook for 8 hours on Low. Se warm.

Nutrition:

- Info Per Serving: Calories: 300;Fat: 10g;Prote 38g;Carbs: 26g.

Beef Cherry & Tomato Cassoulet

Servings:4
Cooking Time:30 Minutes
Ingredients:

- 3 tbsp olive oil
- 2 garlic cloves, minced
- 1 lemon, juiced and zested
- 1 ½ lb ground beef
- Salt and black pepper to taste
- 1 lb cherry tomatoes, halved
- 1 red onion, chopped
- 2 tbsp tomato paste
- 1 tbsp mint leaves, chopped

Directions:

1. Warm the olive oil in a skillet over medium h and cook beef and garlic for 5 minutes. Stir in lem zest, lemon juice, salt, pepper, cherry tomatoes, oni tomato paste, and mint and cook for 15 minutes. Se right away.

Nutrition:

- Info Per Serving: Calories: 324;Fat: 10g;Prote 16g;Carbs: 22g.

Baked Chicken & Veggie

Servings:4
Cooking Time:50 Minutes
Ingredients:

- 4 fresh prunes, cored and quartered
- 2 tbsp olive oil
- 4 chicken legs
- 1 lb baby potatoes, halved
- 1 carrot, julienned
- 2 tbsp chopped fresh parsley
- Salt and black pepper to taste

Directions:

. Preheat oven to 420 F. Combine potatoes, carrot, prunes, olive oil, salt, and pepper in a bowl. Transfer to baking dish. Top with chicken. Season with salt and pepper. Roast for about 40-45 minutes. Serve topped with parsley.

Nutrition:

Info Per Serving: Calories: 473;Fat: 23g;Protein: 1g;Carbs: 49g.

Portuguese-style Chicken Breasts

Servings:4
Cooking Time:45 Minutes
Ingredients:

- 2 tbsp avocado oil
- 1 lb chicken breasts, cubed
- Salt and black pepper to taste
- 1 red onion, chopped
- 15 oz canned chickpeas
- 15 oz canned tomatoes, diced
- 1 cup Kalamata olives, pitted and halved
- 2 tbsp lime juice
- 1 tsp cilantro, chopped

Directions:

. Warm the olive oil in a pot over medium heat and sauté chicken and onion for 5 minutes. Put in salt, pepper, chickpeas, tomatoes, olives, lime juice, cilantro, and 2 cups of water. Cover with lid and bring to a boil, then reduce the heat and simmer for 30 minutes. Serve warm.

Nutrition:

Info Per Serving: Calories: 360;Fat: 16g;Protein: 8g;Carbs: 26g.

Spanish Pork Shoulder

Servings:4
Cooking Time:35 Minutes
Ingredients:

- 3 tbsp olive oil
- 1 ½ lb pork shoulder, cubed
- 2 garlic cloves, minced
- Salt and black pepper to taste
- ½ cup vegetable stock
- ½ tsp saffron powder
- ¼ tsp cumin, ground
- 4 green onions, sliced

Directions:

1. Warm the olive oil in a skillet over medium heat and cook garlic, green onions, saffron, and cumin for 5 minutes. Put in pork and cook for another 5 minutes. Stir in salt, pepper, and stock and bring to a boil. Cook for an additional 15 minutes.

Nutrition:

- Info Per Serving: Calories: 300;Fat: 14g;Protein: 15g;Carbs: 14g.

Chicken With Bell Peppers

Servings:4
Cooking Time:65 Minutes
Ingredients:

- 2 tbsp olive oil
- 2 lb chicken breasts, cubed
- 2 garlic cloves, minced
- 1 red onion, chopped
- 2 red bell peppers, chopped
- ¼ tsp cumin, ground
- 2 cups corn
- ½ cup chicken stock
- 1 tsp chili powder

Directions:

1. Warm the olive oil in a skillet over medium heat and sear chicken for 8 minutes on both sides. Put in onion and garlic and cook for another 5 minutes. Stir in bell peppers, cumin, corn, stock, and chili powder. Cook for 45 minutes. Serve.

Nutrition:

- Info Per Serving: Calories: 340;Fat: 17g;Protein: 19g;Carbs: 27g.

Chicken Thighs With Roasted Artichokes

Servings:4
Cooking Time:25 Minutes
Ingredients:
- 2 artichoke hearts, halved lengthwise
- 2 tbsp butter, melted
- 3 tbsp olive oil
- 2 lemons, zested and juiced
- ½ tsp salt
- 4 chicken thighs

Directions:
1. Preheat oven to 450 F. Place a large, rimmed baking sheet in the oven. Whisk the olive oil, lemon zest, and lemon juice in a bowl. Add the artichoke hearts and turn them to coat on all sides. Lay the artichoke halves flat-side down in the center of 4 aluminum foil sheets and close up loosely to create packets. Put the chicken in the remaining lemon mixture and toss to coat. Carefully remove the hot baking sheet from the oven and pour on the butter; tilt the pan to coat.
2. Arrange the chicken thighs, skin-side down, on the sheet, add the artichoke packets. Roast for about 20 minutes or until the chicken is cooked through and the skin is slightly charred. Check the artichokes for doneness and bake for another 5 minutes if needed. Serve and enjoy!

Nutrition:
- Info Per Serving: Calories: 832;Fat: 80g;Protein: 19g;Carbs: 11g.

Paprika Chicken With Caper Dressing

Servings:4
Cooking Time:35 Minutes
Ingredients:
- 2 tbsp canola oil
- 4 chicken breast halves
- Salt and black pepper to taste
- 1 tbsp sweet paprika
- 1 onion, chopped
- 1 tbsp balsamic vinegar
- 2 tbsp parsley, chopped
- 1 avocado, peeled and cubed
- 2 tbsp capers

Directions:

1. Preheat the grill over medium heat. Rub chicke halves with half of the canola oil, paprika, salt, an pepper and grill them for 14 minutes on both side Share into plates. Combine onion, remaining oi vinegar, parsley, avocado, and capers in a bowl. Pou the sauce over the chicken and serve.

Nutrition:
- Info Per Serving: Calories: 300;Fat: 13g;Protei 15g;Carbs: 25g.

Baked Teriyaki Turkey Meatballs

Servings:6
Cooking Time: 20 Minutes
Ingredients:
- 1 pound lean ground turkey
- 1 egg, whisked
- ¼ cup finely chopped scallions, both white an green parts
- 2 garlic cloves, minced
- 2 tablespoons reduced-sodium tamari or glute free soy sauce
- 1 teaspoon grated fresh ginger
- 1 tablespoon honey
- 2 teaspoons mirin
- 1 teaspoon olive oil

Directions:
1. Preheat the oven to 400°F. Line a baking she with parchment paper and set aside.
2. Mix together the ground turkey, whisked eg scallions, garlic, tamari, ginger, honey, mirin, and oli oil in a large bowl, and stir until well blended.
3. Using a tablespoon to scoop out rounded heaps the turkey mixture, and then roll them into balls wi your hands. Transfer the balls to the prepared bakir sheet.
4. Bake in the preheated oven for 20 minutes, flippir the balls with a spatula halfway through, or until th meatballs are browned and cooked through.
5. Serve warm.

Nutrition:
- Info Per Serving: Calories: 158;Fat: 8.6g;Protei 16.2g;Carbs: 4.0g.

ork Chops With Green Vegetables

Servings:4
Cooking Time:70 Minutes
Ingredients:
- 2 tbsp olive oil, divided
- ½ lb green beans, trimmed
- ½ lb asparagus spears
- ½ cup frozen peas, thawed
- 2 tomatoes, chopped
- 1 lb pork chops
- 1 tbsp tomato paste
- 1 onion, chopped
- Salt and black pepper to taste

Directions:
Warm olive oil in a saucepan over medium heat. Sprinkle the chops with salt and pepper. Place in the pan and brown for 8 minutes in total; set aside. In the same pan, sauté onion for 2 minutes until soft. In a bowl, whisk the tomato paste and 1 cup of water and pour in the saucepan. Bring to a simmer and scrape any bits from the bottom. Add the chops back and bring to a boil. Then lower the heat and simmer for 40 minutes. Add in green beans, asparagus, peas, tomatoes, salt, and pepper and cook for 10 minutes until the greens are soft.

Nutrition:
Info Per Serving: Calories: 341;Fat: 16g;Protein: g;Carbs: 15g.

arsley-dijon Chicken And otatoes

Servings:6
Cooking Time: 22 Minutes
Ingredients:
- 1 tablespoon extra-virgin olive oil
- 1½ pounds boneless, skinless chicken thighs, cut to 1-inch cubes, patted dry
- 1½ pounds Yukon Gold potatoes, unpeeled, cut to ½-inch cubes
- 2 garlic cloves, minced
- ¼ cup dry white wine
- 1 cup low-sodium or no-salt-added chicken broth
- 1 tablespoon Dijon mustard
- ¼ teaspoon freshly ground black pepper
- ¼ teaspoon kosher or sea salt
- 1 cup chopped fresh flat-leaf (Italian) parsley, cluding stems
- 1 tablespoon freshly squeezed lemon juice

Directions:
1. In a large skillet over medium-high heat, heat the oil. Add the chicken and cook for 5 minutes, stirring only after the chicken has browned on one side. Remove the chicken and reserve on a plate.
2. Add the potatoes to the skillet and cook for 5 minutes, stirring only after the potatoes have become golden and crispy on one side. Push the potatoes to the side of the skillet, add the garlic, and cook, stirring constantly, for 1 minute. Add the wine and cook for 1 minute, until nearly evaporated. Add the chicken broth, mustard, salt, pepper, and reserved chicken. Turn the heat to high and bring to a boil.
3. Once boiling, cover, reduce the heat to medium-low, and cook for 10 to 12 minutes, until the potatoes are tender and the internal temperature of the chicken measures 165ºF on a meat thermometer and any juices run clear.
4. During the last minute of cooking, stir in the parsley. Remove from the heat, stir in the lemon juice, and serve.

Nutrition:
- Info Per Serving: Calories: 324;Fat: 9.0g;Protein: 16.0g;Carbs: 45.0g.

Carrot, Potato & Chicken Bake

Servings:4
Cooking Time:60 Minutes
Ingredients:
- 2 tbsp olive oil
- 1 lb chicken breasts, cubed
- 1 carrot, chopped
- 2 garlic cloves, minced
- Salt and black pepper to taste
- 2 tsp thyme, dried
- 1 baby potatoes, halved
- 1 onion, sliced
- ¾ cup chicken stock
- 2 tbsp basil, chopped

Directions:
1. Preheat the oven to 380 F. Grease a baking dish with oil. Put carrot, potatoes, chicken, garlic, salt, pepper, thyme, onion, stock, and basil in the dish and bake for 50 minutes. Serve.

Nutrition:
- Info Per Serving: Calories: 290;Fat: 10g;Protein: 15g;Carbs: 23g.

Tuscan Pork Cassoulet

Servings:4
Cooking Time:30 Minutes
Ingredients:
- 2 tbsp olive oil
- 2 lb pork loin, sliced
- 4 garlic cloves, minced
- 1 cup green olives, halved
- 1 tbsp capers
- ½ cup tomato puree
- Salt and black pepper to taste
- 2 tbsp parsley, chopped
- Juice of 1 lime

Directions:
1. Warm the olive oil in a skillet over medium heat and cook garlic and pork for 5 minutes. Stir in green olives, capers, tomato purée, salt, pepper, parsley, and lime juice and bring to a simmer. Cook for another 15 minutes. Serve.

Nutrition:
- Info Per Serving: Calories: 260;Fat: 13g;Protein: 14g;Carbs: 22g.

Grilled Beef With Mint-jalapeño Vinaigrette

Servings:4
Cooking Time:25 Minutes
Ingredients:
- 2 tbsp olive oil
- 1 lb beef steaks
- 3 jalapeños, chopped
- 2 tbsp balsamic vinegar
- 1 cup mint leaves, chopped
- Salt and black pepper to taste
- 1 tbsp sweet paprika

Directions:
1. Warm half of oil in a skillet over medium heat and sauté jalapeños, balsamic vinegar, mint, salt, pepper, and paprika for 5 minutes. Preheat the grill to high. Rub beef steaks with the remaining oil, salt, and pepper and grill for 6 minutes on both sides. Top with mint vinaigrette and serve.

Nutrition:
- Info Per Serving: Calories: 320;Fat: 13g;Protein: 18g;Carbs: 19g.

Easy Pork Stew(2)

Servings:4
Cooking Time:35 Minutes
Ingredients:
- 2 tbsp olive oil
- 1 lb pork shoulder, cubed
- Salt and black pepper to taste
- 1 onion, chopped
- 2 garlic cloves, minced
- 1 tbsp chili paste
- 2 tbsp balsamic vinegar
- ¼ cup chicken stock
- ¼ cup mint, chopped

Directions:
1. Warm the olive oil in a skillet over medium he and cook onion for 3 minutes. Put in pork cubes a cook for another 3 minutes. Stir in salt, pepper, gar chili paste, vinegar, stock, and mint and cook for additional 20-25 minutes.

Nutrition:
- Info Per Serving: Calories: 310;Fat: 14g;Prote 20g;Carbs: 16g.

Cilantro Turkey Penne With Asparagus

Servings:4
Cooking Time:40 Minutes
Ingredients:
- 3 tbsp olive oil
- 16 oz penne pasta
- 1 lb turkey breast strips
- 1 lb asparagus, chopped
- 1 tsp basil, chopped
- Salt and black pepper to taste
- ½ cup tomato sauce
- 2 tbsp cilantro, chopped

Directions:
1. Bring to a boil salted water in a pot over medi heat and cook penne until "al dente", 8-10 minu Drain and set aside; reserve 1 cup of the cooking wat
2. Warm the olive oil in a skillet over medium h and sear turkey for 4 minutes, stirring periodica Add in asparagus and sauté for 3-4 more minutes. P in the tomato sauce and reserved pasta liquid bring to a boil; simmer for 20 minutes. Stir in coo penne, season with salt and pepper, and top with basil and cilantro to serve.

Nutrition:
- Info Per Serving: Calories: 350;Fat: 22g;Prote 19g;Carbs: 23g.

Eggplant & Chicken Skillet

Servings:4
Cooking Time:40 Minutes
Ingredients:

- 2 tbsp olive oil
- 1 lb eggplants, cubed
- Salt and black pepper to taste
- 1 onion, chopped
- 2 garlic cloves, minced
- 1 tsp hot paprika
- 1 tbsp oregano, chopped
- 1 cup chicken stock
- 1 lb chicken breasts, cubed
- 1 cup half and half
- 3 tsp toasted chopped almonds

Directions:

1. Warm the olive oil in a skillet over medium heat and sauté chicken for 8 minutes, stirring often. Mix in eggplants, onion, and garlic and cook for another 5 minutes. Season with salt, pepper, hot paprika, and oregano and pour in the stock. Bring to a boil and simmer for 16 minutes. Stir in half and half for 2 minutes. Serve topped with almonds.

Nutrition:

- Info Per Serving: Calories: 400;Fat: 13g;Protein: 16g;Carbs: 22g.

Paprika Broccoli & Lamb

Servings:4
Cooking Time:70 Minutes
Ingredients:

- 2 tbsp olive oil
- 1 lb lamb meat, cubed
- 1 garlic clove, minced
- 1 onion, chopped
- 1 tsp rosemary, chopped
- 1 cup vegetable stock
- 2 cups broccoli florets
- 2 tbsp sweet paprika
- Salt and black pepper to taste

Directions:

1. Warm the olive oil in a skillet over medium heat and cook onion and garlic for 5 minutes. Put in lamb meat and cook for another 5-6 minutes. Stir in rosemary, stock, broccoli, paprika, salt, and pepper and cook for 50 minutes. Serve hot.

Nutrition:

- Info Per Serving: Calories: 350;Fat: 16g;Protein: 24g;Carbs: 23g.

Creamy Beef Stew

Servings:4
Cooking Time:35 Minutes
Ingredients:

- 2 tbsp olive oil
- 2 pears, peeled and cubed
- 1 lb beef stew meat, cubed
- 2 tbsp dill, chopped
- 2 oz heavy cream
- Salt and black pepper to taste

Directions:

1. Warm the olive oil in a skillet over medium heat and sear beef for 5 minutes. Stir in pears, dill, heavy cream, salt, and pepper and bring to a boil. Simmer for 20 minutes.

Nutrition:

- Info Per Serving: Calories: 340;Fat: 18g;Protein: 16g;Carbs: 23g.

Chicken With Farro & Carrots

Servings:4
Cooking Time:50 Minutes
Ingredients:

- 2 tbsp olive oil
- 3 carrots, chopped
- 1 cup farro, soaked
- 1 lb chicken breasts, cubed
- 1 red onion, chopped
- 4 garlic cloves, minced
- 2 tbsp dill, chopped
- 2 tbsp tomato paste
- 2 cups vegetable stock
- Salt and black pepper to taste

Directions:

1. Warm olive oil in your pressure cooker on Sauté and sear the chicken for 10 minutes on all sides, stirring occasionally. Remove to a plate. Add onion, garlic, and carrots to the cooker and sauté for 3 minutes. Stir in tomato paste, farro, and vegetable stock and return the chicken. Seal the lid, select Pressure Cook, and cook for 30 minutes on High. Do a natural pressure release for 10 minutes. Adjust the taste with salt and pepper. Sprinkle with dill and serve.

Nutrition:

- Info Per Serving: Calories: 317;Fat: 13g;Protein: 8g;Carbs: 18g.

Juicy Almond Turkey

Servings:4
Cooking Time:40 Minutes
Ingredients:

- 2 tbsp canola oil
- ¼ cup almonds, chopped
- 1 lb turkey breast, sliced
- Salt and black pepper to taste
- 1 lemon, juiced and zested
- 1 grapefruit, juiced
- 1 tbsp rosemary, chopped
- 3 garlic cloves, minced
- 1 cup chicken stock

Directions:

1. Warm the olive oil in a skillet over medium heat and cook garlic and turkey for 8 minutes on both sides. Stir in salt, pepper, lemon juice, lemon zest, grapefruit juice, rosemary, almonds, and stock and bring to a boil. Cook for 20 minutes.

Nutrition:

- Info Per Serving: Calories: 300;Fat: 13g;Protein: 25g;Carbs: 19g.

Authentic Turkey Kofta

Servings:4
Cooking Time:35 Minutes
Ingredients:

- 1 lb ground turkey
- ¼ cup breadcrumbs
- 1 egg
- 2 tbsp hot sauce
- ½ tsp celery seeds
- 2 garlic cloves, minced
- ¼ red onion, chopped
- 2 tbsp chopped fresh mint
- Salt and black pepper to taste

Directions:

1. Preheat oven to 350 F. In a bowl, place turke breadcrumbs, egg, garlic, red onion, mint, hot sauc celery seeds, salt, and pepper. Make small balls out the mixture and arrange them on a lined wi parchment paper baking sheet. Bake for 25 minut until brown. Serve and enjoy!

Nutrition:

- Info Per Serving: Calories: 270;Fat: 14g;Protei 33.6g;Carbs: 6g.

Fruits, Desserts And Snacks Recipes

Hot Italian Sausage Pizza Wraps

Servings:2
Cooking Time:20 Minutes
Ingredients:

- 1 tbsp basil, chopped
- 1 tsp olive oil
- 6 oz spicy Italian sausage
- 1 shallot, chopped
- 1 tsp Italian seasoning
- 4 oz marinara sauce
- 2 flour tortillas
- ½ cup mozzarella, shredded
- 1/3 cup Parmesan, grated
- 1 tsp red pepper flakes

Directions:

1. Warm the olive oil in a skillet over medium hea Add and cook the sausage for 5-6 minutes, stirring a breaking up larger pieces, until cooked throug Remove to a bowl. Sauté the shallot for 3 minutes un soft, stirring frequently. Stir in Italian seasonin marinara sauce, and reserved sausage. Bring to simmer and cook for about 2 minutes. Divide t mixture between the tortillas, top with the cheeses, ac red pepper flakes and basil, and fold over. Ser immediately.

Nutrition:

- Info Per Serving: Calories: 744;Fat: 46g;Protei 41g;Carbs: 40g.

piced Hot Chocolate

rvings:4
oking Time:15 Minutes
gredients:

- ¼ tsp cayenne pepper powder
- 4 squares chocolate
- 4 cups milk
- 2 tsp sugar
- ½ tsp ground cinnamon
- ½ tsp salt

rections:

Place milk and sugar in a pot over low heat and
rm until it begins to simmer.

Combine chocolate, cinnamon, salt, and cayenne
pper powder in a bowl. Slowly pour in enough hot
lk to cover. Return the pot to the heat and lower the
mperature. Stir until the chocolate has melted, then
d the remaining milk and combine. Spoon into 4
ps and serve hot.

utrition:

Info Per Serving: Calories: 342;Fat: 23g;Protein:
g;Carbs: 22g.

imple Apple Compote

rvings:4
oking Time: 10 Minutes
gredients:

- 6 apples, peeled, cored, and chopped
- ¼ cup raw honey
- 1 teaspoon ground cinnamon
- ¼ cup apple juice
- Sea salt, to taste

rections:

Put all the ingredients in a stockpot. Stir to mix
ll, then cook over medium-high heat for 10 minutes
until the apples are glazed by honey and lightly
ucy. Stir constantly.

Serve immediately.

utrition:

Info Per Serving: Calories: 246;Fat: 0.9g;Protein:
g;Carbs: 66.3g.

hyme Lentil Spread

rvings:6
oking Time:10 Minutes
gredients:

- 3 tbsp olive oil
- 1 garlic clove, minced

- 1 cup split red lentils, rinsed
- ½ tsp dried thyme
- 1 tbsp balsamic vinegar
- Salt and black pepper to taste

Directions:

1. Bring to a boil salted water in a pot over medium
heat. Add in the lentils and cook for 15 minutes until
cooked through. Drain and set aside to cool. In a food
processor, place the lentils, garlic, thyme, vinegar, salt,
and pepper. Gradually add olive oil while blending
until smooth. Serve.

Nutrition:

- Info Per Serving: Calories: 295;Fat: 10g;Protein:
10g;Carbs: 16g.

Vegetarian Spinach-olive Pizza

Servings:4
Cooking Time:40 Minutes
Ingredients:

- For the crust
- 1 tbsp olive oil
- ½ cup almond flour
- ¼ tsp salt
- 2 tbsp ground psyllium husk
- 1 cup lukewarm water
- For the topping
- ½ cup tomato sauce
- ½ cup baby spinach
- 1 cup grated mozzarella
- 1 tsp dried oregano
- 3 tbsp sliced black olives

Directions:

1. Preheat the oven to 400 F. Line a baking sheet with
parchment paper. In a medium bowl, mix the almond
flour, salt, psyllium powder, olive oil, and water until
dough forms.

2. Spread the mixture on the pizza pan and bake in
the oven until crusty, 10 minutes. When ready, remove
the crust and spread the tomato sauce on top. Add the
spinach, mozzarella cheese, oregano, and olives. Bake
until the cheese melts, 15 minutes. Take out of the oven,
slice and serve warm.

Nutrition:

- Info Per Serving: Calories: 167;Fat: 13g;Protein:
4g;Carbs: 6.7g.

Chocolate-avocado Cream

Servings:4
Cooking Time:10 Min + Chilling Time
Ingredients:
- 2 avocados, mashed
- ¼ cup cocoa powder
- ¼ cup heavy whipping cream
- 2 tsp vanilla extract
- 2 tbsp sugar
- ½ tsp ground cinnamon
- ¼ tsp salt

Directions:
1. Blend the avocado, cocoa powder, heavy whipping cream, vanilla, sugar, cinnamon, and salt into a large bowl until smooth and creamy. Cover and refrigerate for at least 1 hour.

Nutrition:
- Info Per Serving: Calories: 230;Fat: 22g;Protein: 3g;Carbs: 10g.

Fruit Skewers With Vanilla Labneh

Servings:4
Cooking Time:15 Min + Straining Time
Ingredients:
- 2 cups plain yogurt
- 2 tbsp honey
- 1 tsp vanilla extract
- A pinch of salt
- 2 mangoes, cut into chunks

Directions:
1. Place a fine sieve lined with cheesecloth over a bowl and spoon the yogurt into the sieve. Allow the liquid to drain off for 12-24 hours hours. Transfer the strained yogurt to a bowl and mix in the honey, vanilla, and salt. Set it aside.
2. Heat your grill to medium-high. Thread the fruit onto skewers and grill for 2 minutes on each side until the fruit is softened and has grill marks on each side. Serve with labneh.

Nutrition:
- Info Per Serving: Calories: 292;Fat: 6g;Protein: 5g;Carbs: 60g.

Grilled Stone Fruit With Honey

Servings:2
Cooking Time: 6 Minutes
Ingredients:
- 3 apricots, halved and pitted
- 2 plums, halved and pitted
- 2 peaches, halved and pitted

- ½ cup low-fat ricotta cheese
- 2 tablespoons honey
- Cooking spray

Directions:
1. Preheat the grill to medium heat. Spray the g grates with cooking spray.
2. Arrange the fruit, cut side down, on the grill, a cook for 2 to 3 minutes per side, or until lightly char and softened.
3. Serve warm with a sprinkle of cheese and a driz of honey.

Nutrition:
- Info Per Serving: Calories: 298;Fat: 7.8g;Prote 11.9g;Carbs: 45.2g.

Mini Nuts And Fruits Crumble

Servings:6
Cooking Time: 15 Minutes
Ingredients:
- Topping:
- ¼ cup coarsely chopped hazelnuts
- 1 cup coarsely chopped walnuts
- 1 teaspoon ground cinnamon
- Sea salt, to taste
- 1 tablespoon melted coconut oil
- Filling:
- 6 fresh figs, quartered
- 2 nectarines, pitted and sliced
- 1 cup fresh blueberries
- 2 teaspoons lemon zest
- ½ cup raw honey
- 1 teaspoon vanilla extract

Directions:
1. Make the Topping:
2. Combine the ingredients for the topping in a bo Stir to mix well. Set aside until ready to use.
3. Make the Filling:
4. Preheat the oven to 375°F.
5. Combine the ingredients for the fillings in a bo Stir to mix well.
6. Divide the filling in six ramekins, then divide a top with nut topping.
7. Bake in the preheated oven for 15 minutes or u the topping is lightly browned and the filling is froth
8. Serve immediately.

Nutrition:
- Info Per Serving: Calories: 336;Fat: 18.8g;Prote 6.3g;Carbs: 41.9g.

Cinnamon Pear & Oat Crisp With Pecans

Servings:4

Cooking Time:30 Minutes

Ingredients:

- 2 tbsp butter, melted
- 4 fresh pears, mashed
- ½ lemon, juiced and zested
- ¼ cup maple syrup
- 1 cup gluten-free rolled oats
- ½ cup chopped pecans
- ½ tsp ground cinnamon
- ¼ tsp salt

Directions:

. Preheat oven to 350 F. Combine the pears, lemon juice and zest, and maple syrup in a bowl. Stir to mix well, then spread the mixture on a greased baking dish. Combine the remaining ingredients in a small bowl. Stir to mix well. Pour the mixture over the pear mixture. Bake for 20 minutes or until the oats are golden brown.

Nutrition:

Info Per Serving: Calories: 496;Fat: 33g;Protein: g;Carbs: 50.8g.

Stuffed Cucumber Bites

Servings:4

Cooking Time:10 Minutes

Ingredients:

- ¼ cup extra-virgin olive oil
- 2 cucumbers
- Salt to taste
- 6 basil leaves, chopped
- 1 tbsp fresh mint, minced
- 1 garlic clove, minced
- ¼ cup walnuts, ground
- ¼ cup feta cheese, crumbled
- ½ tsp paprika

Directions:

. Cut cucumbers lengthwise. With a spoon, remove the seeds and hollow out a shallow trough in each piece. Lightly salt each piece and set aside on a platter. In a bowl, combine the basil, mint, garlic, walnuts, feta, and olive oil and blend until smooth. Spoon the mixture into each cucumber half and sprinkle with paprika. Cut each half into 4 pieces. Serve.

Nutrition:

- Info Per Serving: Calories: 176;Fat: 3g;Protein: 5g;Carbs: 18g.

Stuffed Cherry Tomatoes

Servings:4

Cooking Time:10 Minutes

Ingredients:

- 2 tbsp olive oil
- 16 cherry tomatoes
- 1 tbsp lemon zest
- ½ cup feta cheese, crumbled
- 2 tbsp olive tapenade
- ¼ cup parsley, torn

Directions:

1. Using a sharp knife, slice off the tops of the tomatoes and hollow out the insides. Combine olive oil, lemon zest, feta cheese, olive tapenade, and parsley in a bowl. Fill the cherry tomatoes with the feta mixture and arrange them on a plate.

Nutrition:

- Info Per Serving: Calories: 140;Fat: 9g;Protein: 6g;Carbs: 6g.

Classic Tzatziki Dip

Servings:6

Cooking Time:10 Min + Chilling Time

Ingredients:

- 1 large cucumber, grated
- 1 garlic clove, minced
- 1 cup Greek yogurt
- 1 tsp chopped fresh dill
- 1 tsp chopped fresh parsley
- Salt and black pepper to taste
- ¼ cup ground walnuts

Directions:

1. In a colander over the sink, squeeze the excess liquid out of the grated cucumber. Combine the yogurt, cucumber, garlic, salt, dill, and pepper in a bowl. Keep in the fridge covered for 2 hours. Serve topped with ground walnuts and parsley.

Nutrition:

- Info Per Serving: Calories: 66;Fat: 3.8g;Protein: 5g;Carbs: 4g.

Crunchy Almond Cookies

Servings:4
Cooking Time: 5 To 7 Minutes
Ingredients:
- ½ cup sugar
- 8 tablespoons almond butter
- 1 large egg
- 1½ cups all-purpose flour
- 1 cup ground almonds

Directions:
1. Preheat the oven to 375°F. Line a baking sheet with parchment paper.
2. Using a mixer, whisk together the sugar and butter. Add the egg and mix until combined. Alternately add the flour and ground almonds, ½ cup at a time, while the mixer is on slow.
3. Drop 1 tablespoon of the dough on the prepared baking sheet, keeping the cookies at least 2 inches apart.
4. Put the baking sheet in the oven and bake for about 5 to 7 minutes, or until the cookies start to turn brown around the edges.
5. Let cool for 5 minutes before serving.

Nutrition:
- Info Per Serving: Calories: 604;Fat: 36.0g;Protein: 11.0g;Carbs: 63.0g.

Orange Mug Cakes

Servings:2
Cooking Time: 3 Minutes
Ingredients:
- 6 tablespoons flour
- 2 tablespoons sugar
- 1 teaspoon orange zest
- ½ teaspoon baking powder
- Pinch salt
- 1 egg
- 2 tablespoons olive oil
- 2 tablespoons unsweetened almond milk
- 2 tablespoons freshly squeezed orange juice
- ½ teaspoon orange extract
- ½ teaspoon vanilla extract

Directions:
1. Combine the flour, sugar, orange zest, baking powder, and salt in a small bowl.
2. In another bowl, whisk together the egg, olive oil, milk, orange juice, orange extract, and vanilla extract.
3. Add the dry ingredients to the wet ingredients and stir to incorporate. The batter will be thick.
4. Divide the mixture into two small mugs. Microwave each mug separately. The small ones should

take about 60 seconds, and one large mug should take about 90 seconds, but microwaves can vary.
5. Cool for 5 minutes before serving.
Nutrition:
- Info Per Serving: Calories: 303;Fat: 16.9g;Protein 6.0g;Carbs: 32.5g.

Dates Stuffed With Mascarpone & Almonds

Servings:6
Cooking Time:10 Minutes
Ingredients:
- 20 blanched almonds
- 8 oz mascarpone cheese
- 20 Medjool dates
- 2 tbsp honey

Directions:
1. Using a knife, cut one side of the date lengthwise from the stem to the bottom. Gently remove the stone and replace it with a blanched almond. Spoon the cheese into a piping bag. Squeeze a generous amount of the cheese into each date. Set the dates on a serving plate and drizzle with honey. Serve immediately or chill in the fridge.

Nutrition:
- Info Per Serving: Calories: 253;Fat: 15g;Protein 2g;Carbs: 31g.

Homemade Studentenfutter

Servings:4
Cooking Time:10 Minutes
Ingredients:
- ¼ cup dried figs
- ½ cup almonds
- ¼ seed mix
- ¼ cup dried cranberries
- ½ cup walnut halves
- ½ cup hazelnuts
- ½ tsp paprika
- 1 tbsp Parmesan cheese, grated

Directions:
1. Spread the almonds, walnuts, hazelnuts, and seeds on a greased baking dish. Bake in preheated oven for 10 minutes at 350 F. Remove and mix with figs and cranberries. Toss to combine. Sprinkle with Parmesan and paprika and serve.

Nutrition:
- Info Per Serving: Calories: 195;Fat: 15.6g;Protein 7g;Carbs: 9.8g.

Banana, Cranberry, And Oat Bars

Servings:16
Cooking Time: 40 Minutes
Ingredients:

 2 tablespoon extra-virgin olive oil

 2 medium ripe bananas, mashed

 ½ cup almond butter

 ½ cup maple syrup

 ⅓ cup dried cranberries

 1½ cups old-fashioned rolled oats

 ¼ cup oat flour

 ¼ cup ground flaxseed

 ¼ teaspoon ground cloves

 ½ cup shredded coconut

 ½ teaspoon ground cinnamon

 1 teaspoon vanilla extract

Directions:

Preheat the oven to 400°F. Line a 8-inch square pan with parchment paper, then grease with olive oil.

Combine the mashed bananas, almond butter, and maple syrup in a bowl. Stir to mix well.

Mix in the remaining ingredients and stir to mix well until thick and sticky.

Spread the mixture evenly on the square pan with a spatula, then bake in the preheated oven for 40 minutes or until a toothpick inserted in the center comes out clean.

Remove them from the oven and slice into 16 bars serve.

Nutrition:

Info Per Serving: Calories: 145;Fat: 7.2g;Protein: 1g;Carbs: 18.9g.

Pomegranate Blueberry Granita

Servings:2
Cooking Time:15 Min + Freezing Time
Ingredients:

 1 cup blueberries

 1 cup pomegranate juice

 ¼ cup sugar

 ¼ tsp lemon zest

Directions:

Place the blueberries, lemon zest, and pomegranate juice in a saucepan over medium heat and bring to a boil. Simmer for 5 minutes or until the blueberries start to break down. Stir the sugar in ¼ cup of water until the sugar is dissolved. Place the blueberry mixture and the sugar water in your blender and blitz for 1 minute or until the fruit is puréed.

2. Pour the mixture into a baking pan. The liquid should come about ½ inch up the sides. Let the mixture cool for 30 minutes, and then put it into the freezer. Every 30 minutes for the next 2 hours, scrape the granita with a fork to keep it from freezing solid. Serve it after 2 hours, or store it in a covered container in the freezer.

Nutrition:

 Info Per Serving: Calories: 214;Fat: 0g;Protein: 1g;Carbs: 54g.

Vegetarian Patties

Servings:4
Cooking Time:20 Minutes
Ingredients:

  3 tbsp olive oil

  2 carrots, grated

  2 zucchinis, grated and drained

  2 garlic cloves, minced

  2 spring onions, chopped

  1 tsp cumin

  ½ tsp turmeric powder

  Salt and black pepper to taste

  ¼ tsp ground coriander

  2 tbsp parsley, chopped

  ¼ tsp lemon juice

  ½ cup flour

  1 egg, whisked

  ¼ cup breadcrumbs

Directions:

1. Combine garlic, spring onions, carrot, cumin, turmeric, salt, pepper, coriander, parsley, lemon juice, flour, zucchinis, egg, and breadcrumbs in a bowl and mix well. Form balls out of the mixture and flatten them to form patties.

2. Warm olive oil in a skillet over medium heat. Fry the cakes for 10 minutes on both sides. Remove to a paper-lined plate to drain the excessive grease. Serve warm.

Nutrition:

 Info Per Serving: Calories: 220;Fat: 12g;Protein: 5g;Carbs: 5g.

Mini Meatball Pizza

Servings:4
Cooking Time:25 Minutes
Ingredients:

- 1 pizza crust
- 1 ½ cups pizza sauce
- ½ tsp dried oregano
- 8 oz bite-sized meatballs
- 1 cup bell peppers, sliced
- 2 cups mozzarella, shredded

Directions:

1. Preheat oven to 400 F. Spread the pizza crust evenly with pizza sauce and sprinkle with oregano. Arrange the meatballs on the pizza sauce. Sprinkle with bell peppers and mozzarella cheese. Bake for about 20 minutes or until the crust is golden brown and cheese melts. Serve immediately.

Nutrition:

- Info Per Serving: Calories: 555;Fat: 28g;Protein: 30g;Carbs: 45g.

Olive Mezze Platter

Servings:2
Cooking Time:10 Min + Marinating Time
Ingredients:

- 2 cups mixed green olives with pits
- ¼ cup extra-virgin olive oil
- ¼ cup red wine vinegar
- 1 tsp dried oregano
- 1 orange, zested and juiced
- ½ tsp crushed chilies
- ½ tsp ground cumin

Directions:

1. Combine the olives, vinegar, olive oil, garlic, oregano, crushed chilies, and cumin in a large glass and mix well. Cover and set aside to marinate for 30 minutes. Keep for up to 14 days in the refrigerator.

Nutrition:

- Info Per Serving: Calories: 133;Fat: 14g;Protein: 1g;Carbs: 3g.

Raspberry Yogurt Basted Cantaloupe

Servings:6
Cooking Time: 0 Minutes
Ingredients:

- 2 cups fresh raspberries, mashed
- 1 cup plain coconut yogurt
- ½ teaspoon vanilla extract
- 1 cantaloupe, peeled and sliced
- ½ cup toasted coconut flakes

Directions:

1. Combine the mashed raspberries with yogurt a vanilla extract in a small bowl. Stir to mix well.

2. Place the cantaloupe slices on a platter, then t with raspberry mixture and spread with toast coconut.

3. Serve immediately.

Nutrition:

- Info Per Serving: Calories: 75;Fat: 4.1g;Prote 1.2g;Carbs: 10.9g.

Cozy Superfood Hot Chocolate

Servings:2
Cooking Time: 8 Minutes
Ingredients:

- 2 cups unsweetened almond milk
- 1 tablespoon avocado oil
- 1 tablespoon collagen protein powder
- 2 teaspoons coconut sugar
- 2 tablespoons cocoa powder
- 1 teaspoon ground cinnamon
- 1 teaspoon ground ginger
- 1 teaspoon vanilla extract
- ½ teaspoon ground turmeric
- Dash salt
- Dash cayenne pepper (optional)

Directions:

1. In a small saucepan over medium heat, warm almond milk and avocado oil for about 7 minu stirring frequently.

2. Fold in the protein powder, which will o properly dissolve in a heated liquid.

3. Stir in the coconut sugar and cocoa powder u melted and dissolved. Carefully transfer the wa liquid into a blender, along with the cinnamon, gin vanilla, turmeric, salt, and cayenne pepper (if desir Blend for 15 seconds until frothy.

4. Serve immediately.

Nutrition:

- Info Per Serving: Calories: 217;Fat: 11.0g;Prote 11.2g;Carbs: 14.8g.

Italian Popcorn

Servings:6
Cooking Time:20 Minutes
Ingredients:
- 2 tbsp butter, melted
- 1 tbsp truffle oil
- 8 cups air-popped popcorn
- 2 tbsp packed brown sugar
- 2 tbsp Italian seasoning
- ¼ tsp sea salt

Directions:
. Preheat oven to 350 F. Combine butter, Italian seasoning, sugar, and salt in a bowl. Pour over the popcorn and toss well to coat. Remove to a baking dish and bake for 15 minutes, stirring frequently. Drizzle with truffle oil and serve.

Nutrition:
- Info Per Serving: Calories: 80;Fat: 5g;Protein: .1g;Carbs: 8.4g.

Shallot & Kale Spread

Servings:4
Cooking Time:10 Minutes
Ingredients:
- 2 shallots, chopped
- 1 lb kale, roughly chopped
- 2 tbsp mint, chopped
- ¾ cup cream cheese, soft
- Salt and black pepper to taste

Directions:
. In a food processor, blend kale, shallots, mint, cream cheese, salt, and pepper until smooth. Serve.

Nutrition:
- Info Per Serving: Calories: 210;Fat: 12g;Protein: g;Carbs: 5g.

Avocado & Dark Chocolate Mousse

Servings:4
Cooking Time:10 Min + Freezing Time
Ingredients:
- 2 tbsp olive oil
- 8 oz dark chocolate, chopped
- ¼ cup milk
- 2 ripe avocados, deseeded
- ¼ cup honey
- 1 cup strawberries

Directions:
1. Cook the chocolate, olive oil, and milk in a saucepan over medium heat for 3 minutes or until the chocolate melt, stirring constantly. Put the avocado in a food processor, then drizzle with honey and melted chocolate. Pulse to combine until smooth. Pour the mixture into a serving bowl, then sprinkle with strawberries. Chill for 30 minutes and serve.

Nutrition:
- Info Per Serving: Calories: 654;Fat: 47g;Protein: 7.2g;Carbs: 56g.

Caramel Peach & Walnut Cake

Servings:6
Cooking Time:50 Min + Cooling Time
Ingredients:
- ¼ cup coconut oil
- ¼ cup olive oil
- 2 peeled peaches, chopped
- ½ cup raisins, soaked
- 1 cup plain flour
- 3 eggs
- 1 tbsp dark rum
- ¼ tsp ground cinnamon
- 1 tsp vanilla extract
- 1 ½ tsp baking powder
- 4 tbsp Greek yogurt
- 2 tbsp honey
- 1 cup brown sugar
- 4 tbsp walnuts, chopped
- ¼ caramel sauce
- ¼ tsp salt

Directions:
1. Preheat the oven to 350 F. In a bowl, mix the flour, cinnamon, vanilla, baking powder, and salt. In another bowl, whisk the eggs with Greek yogurt using an electric mixer. Gently add in coconut and olive oil. Combine well. Put in rum, honey and sugar; stir to combine. Mix the wet ingredients with the dry mixture. Stir in peaches, raisins, and walnuts.

2. Pour the mixture into a greased baking pan and bake for 30-40 minutes until a knife inserted into the middle of the cake comes out clean. Remove from the oven and let sit for 10 minutes, then invert onto a wire rack to cool completely. Warm the caramel sauce through in a pan and pour it over the cooled cake to serve.

Nutrition:
- Info Per Serving: Calories: 568;Fat: 26g;Protein: 215g;Carbs: 66g.

Cucumber Noodles With Goat Cheese

Servings:4
Cooking Time:5 Minutes
Ingredients:
- ½ cup olive oil
- 2 cucumbers, spiralized
- ½ cup black olives, sliced
- 12 cherry tomatoes, halved
- Salt and black pepper to taste
- 1 small red onion, chopped
- ½ cup goat cheese, crumbled
- ¼ cup apple cider vinegar

Directions:
1. Combine olives, tomatoes, salt, pepper, onion, goat cheese, olive oil, and vinegar in a bowl and mix well. Place the cucumbers on a platter and top with the cheese mixture.

Nutrition:
- Info Per Serving: Calories: 150;Fat: 15g;Protein: 2g;Carbs: 4g.

Apple And Berries Ambrosia

Servings:4
Cooking Time: 0 Minutes
Ingredients:
- 2 cups unsweetened coconut milk, chilled
- 2 tablespoons raw honey
- 1 apple, peeled, cored, and chopped
- 2 cups fresh raspberries
- 2 cups fresh blueberries

Directions:
1. Spoon the chilled milk in a large bowl, then mix in the honey. Stir to mix well.
2. Then mix in the remaining ingredients. Stir to coat the fruits well and serve immediately.

Nutrition:
- Info Per Serving: Calories: 386;Fat: 21.1g;Protein: 4.2g;Carbs: 45.9g.

Greek Yogurt & Za'atar Dip On Grilled Pitta

Servings:6
Cooking Time:10 Minutes
Ingredients:
- 1/3 cup olive oil
- 2 cups Greek yogurt
- 2 tbsp toasted ground pistachios
- Salt and white pepper to taste
- 2 tbsp mint, chopped
- 3 kalamata olives, chopped
- ¼ cup za'atar seasoning
- 3 pitta breads, cut into triangles

Directions:
1. Mix the yogurt, pistachios, salt, pepper, min olives, za'atar spice, and olive oil in a bowl. Grill th pitta bread until golden, about 5-6 minutes. Serve wit the yogurt spread.

Nutrition:
- Info Per Serving: Calories: 300;Fat: 19g;Protei 11g;Carbs: 22g.

Cherry Walnut Brownies

Servings:9
Cooking Time: 20 Minutes
Ingredients:
- 2 large eggs
- ½ cup 2% plain Greek yogurt
- ½ cup sugar
- ⅓ cup honey
- ¼ cup extra-virgin olive oil
- 1 teaspoon vanilla extract
- ½ cup whole-wheat pastry flour
- ⅓ cup unsweetened dark chocolate cocoa powder
- ¼ teaspoon baking powder
- ¼ teaspoon salt
- ⅓ cup chopped walnuts
- 9 fresh cherries, stemmed and pitted
- Cooking spray

Directions:
1. Preheat the oven to 375°F and set the rack in t middle of the oven. Spritz a square baking pan wi cooking spray.
2. In a large bowl, whisk together the eggs, yogu sugar, honey, oil and vanilla.
3. In a medium bowl, stir together the flour, coc powder, baking powder and salt. Add the flour mixtu to the egg mixture and whisk until all the d ingredients are incorporated. Fold in the walnuts.
4. Pour the batter into the prepared pan. Push t cherries into the batter, three to a row in three rows, one will be at the center of each brownie once you c them into squares.
5. Bake the brownies for 20 minutes, or until just s Remove from the oven and place on a rack to cool for minutes. Cut into nine squares and serve.

Nutrition:
- Info Per Serving: Calories: 154;Fat: 6.0g;Protei 3.0g;Carbs: 24.0g.

Fresh Fruit Cups

Servings:4
Cooking Time:10 Minutes
Ingredients:

- 1 cup orange juice
- ½ cup watermelon cubes
- 1 ½ cups grapes, halved
- 1 cup chopped cantaloupe
- ½ cup cherries, chopped
- 1 peach, chopped
- ½ tsp ground cinnamon

Directions:

Combine watermelon cubes, grapes, cherries, cantaloupe, and peach in a bowl. Add in the orange juice and mix well. Share into dessert cups, dust with cinnamon, and serve.

Nutrition:

Info Per Serving: Calories: 156;Fat: 0.5g;Protein: 3g;Carbs: 24g.

Greek Yogurt Affogato With Pistachios

Servings:4
Cooking Time: 0 Minutes
Ingredients:

- 24 ounces vanilla Greek yogurt
- 2 teaspoons sugar
- 4 shots hot espresso
- 4 tablespoons chopped unsalted pistachios
- 4 tablespoons dark chocolate chips

Directions:

Spoon the yogurt into four bowls or tall glasses.

Mix ½ teaspoon of sugar into each of the espresso shots.

Pour one shot of the hot espresso over each bowl of yogurt.

Top each bowl with 1 tablespoon of the pistachios and 1 tablespoon of the chocolate chips and serve.

Nutrition:

Info Per Serving: Calories: 190;Fat: 6.0g;Protein: .0g;Carbs: 14.0g.

Veggie Pizza With Caramelized Onions

Servings:4
Cooking Time:90 Minutes
Ingredients:

- For the crust
- 2 tbsp olive oil
- 2 cups flour
- 1 cup lukewarm water
- 1 pinch of sugar
- 1 tsp active dry yeast
- ¾ tsp salt
- For the caramelized onion
- 2 tbsp olive oil
- 1 onion, sliced
- 1 tsp sugar
- ½ tsp salt
- For the pizza
- ¼ cup shaved Pecorino Romano cheese
- 2 tbsp olive oil
- ½ cup grated mozzarella
- 1 cup baby spinach
- ¼ cup chopped fresh basil
- ½ red bell pepper, sliced

Directions:

1. Sift the flour and salt in a bowl and stir in yeast. Mix lukewarm water, olive oil, and sugar in another bowl. Add the wet mixture to the dry mixture and whisk until you obtain a soft dough. Place the dough on a lightly floured work surface and knead it thoroughly until elastic. Transfer the dough to a greased bowl. Cover with cling film and leave to rise for 50-60 minutes in a warm place until doubled in size. Roll out the dough to a thickness of around 12 inches.

2. Warm olive oil in a skillet over medium heat and sauté onion with salt and sugar for 3 minutes. Lower the heat and brown for 20-35 minutes until caramelized. Preheat oven to 390 F. Transfer the pizza crust to a baking sheet. Drizzle the crust with olive oil and top with onion. Cover with bell pepper and mozzarella. Bake for 10-15 minutes. Serve topped with baby spinach, basil, and Pecorino cheese.

Nutrition:

- Info Per Serving: Calories: 399;Fat: 22.7g;Protein: 8g;Carbs: 43g.

Two-cheese Stuffed Bell Peppers

Servings:6
Cooking Time:20 Min + Chilling Time
Ingredients:

- 1 ½ lb bell peppers, cored and seeded
- 1 tbsp extra-virgin olive oil
- 4 oz ricotta cheese
- 4 oz mascarpone cheese
- 1 tbsp scallions, chopped
- 1 tbsp lemon zest

Directions:

1. Preheat oven to 400 F. Coat the peppers with olive oil, put them on a baking sheet, and roast for 8 minutes. Remove and let cool. In a bowl, add the ricotta cheese, mascarpone cheese, scallions, and lemon zest. Stir to combine, then spoon mixture into a piping bag. Stuff each pepper to the top with the cheese mixture. Chill the peppers and serve.

Nutrition:

- Info Per Serving: Calories: 141;Fat: 11g;Protein: 4g;Carbs: 6g.

Mango And Coconut Frozen Pie

Servings:8
Cooking Time: 0 Minutes
Ingredients:

- Crust:
- 1 cup cashews
- ½ cup rolled oats
- 1 cup soft pitted dates
- Filling:
- 2 large mangoes, peeled and chopped
- ½ cup unsweetened shredded coconut
- 1 cup unsweetened coconut milk
- ½ cup water

Directions:

1. Combine the ingredients for the crust in a food processor. Pulse to combine well.
2. Pour the mixture in an 8-inch springform pan, then press to coat the bottom. Set aside.
3. Combine the ingredients for the filling in the food processor, then pulse to purée until smooth.
4. Pour the filling over the crust, then use a spatula to spread the filling evenly. Put the pan in the freeze for 30 minutes.
5. Remove the pan from the freezer and allow to sit for 15 minutes under room temperature before serving.

Nutrition:

- Info Per Serving: Calories: 426;Fat: 28.2g;Prote 8.1g;Carbs: 14.9g.

Lemony Tea And Chia Pudding

Servings:3
Cooking Time: 0 Minutes
Ingredients:

- 2 teaspoons matcha green tea powder (optional)
- 2 tablespoons ground chia seeds
- 1 to 2 dates
- 2 cups unsweetened coconut milk
- Zest and juice of 1 lime

Directions:

1. Put all the ingredients in a food processor a pulse until creamy and smooth.
2. Pour the mixture in a bowl, then wrap in plast Store in the refrigerator for at least 20 minutes, th serve chilled.

Nutrition:

- Info Per Serving: Calories: 225;Fat: 20.1g;Prote 3.2g;Carbs: 5.9g.

Balsamic Squash Wedges With Walnuts

Servings:4
Cooking Time:50 Minutes
Ingredients:

- 3 tbsp olive oil
- 1 lb butternut squash, peeled and cut into wedge:
- 1 cup walnuts, chopped
- 1 tbsp chili paste
- 1 tbsp balsamic vinegar
- 1 tbsp chives, chopped

Directions:

1. Preheat the oven to 380 F. Line a baking sheet w parchment paper. Combine squash wedges, chili pa: olive oil, vinegar, and chives in a bowl and arrange the sheet. Bake for 40 minutes, turning often. Sprin with walnuts.

Nutrition:

- Info Per Serving: Calories: 190;Fat: 5g;Prote 2g;Carbs: 7g.

Basic Pudding With Kiwi

Servings:4

Cooking Time:20 Min + Chilling Time

Ingredients:

- 2 kiwi, peeled and sliced
- 1 egg
- 2 ¼ cups milk
- ½ cup honey
- 1 tsp vanilla extract
- 3 tbsp cornstarch

Directions:

. In a bowl, beat the egg with honey. Stir in 2 cups of milk and vanilla. Pour into a pot over medium heat and bring to a boil. Combine cornstarch and remaining milk in a bowl. Pour slowly into the pot and boil for 1 minute until thickened, stirring often. Divide between cups and transfer to the fridge. Top with kiwi and serve.

Nutrition:

Info Per Serving: Calories: 262;Fat: 4.1g;Protein: .5g;Carbs: 52g.

Salmon-cucumber Rolls

Servings:4

Cooking Time:5 Minutes

Ingredients:

- 8 Kalamata olives, chopped
- 4 oz smoked salmon strips
- 1 cucumber, sliced lengthwise
- 2 tsp lime juice
- 4 oz cream cheese, soft
- 1 tsp lemon zest, grated
- Salt and black pepper to taste
- 2 tsp dill, chopped

Directions:

. Place cucumber slices on a flat surface and top each with a salmon strip. Combine olives, lime juice, cream cheese, lemon zest, salt, pepper, and dill in a bowl. Smear cream mixture over salmon and roll them up. Serve immediately.

Nutrition:

Info Per Serving: Calories: 250;Fat: 16g;Protein: 8g;Carbs: 17g.

Spiced Fries

Servings:6

Cooking Time:35 Minutes

Ingredients:

- 2 lb red potatoes, cut into wedges
- ¼ cup olive oil
- 3 tbsp garlic, minced
- ½ tsp smoked paprika
- Salt and black pepper to taste
- ½ cup fresh cilantro, chopped
- ¼ tsp cayenne pepper

Directions:

1. Preheat oven to 450 F. Place the potatoes into a bowl. Add the garlic, salt, pepper, and olive oil and toss everything together to coat evenly. Spread the potato mixture onto a baking sheet; bake for 25 minutes, flipping them halfway through the cooking time until golden and crisp. Sprinkle the potatoes with cilantro, cayenne pepper, and smoked paprika. Serve warm and enjoy!

Nutrition:

- Info Per Serving: Calories: 203;Fat: 11g;Protein: 3g;Carbs: 24g.

Cheese Stuffed Potato Skins

Servings:4

Cooking Time:40 Minutes

Ingredients:

- 2 tbsp olive oil
- 1 lb red baby potatoes
- 1 cup ricotta cheese, crumbled
- 2 garlic cloves, minced
- 1 tbsp chives, chopped
- ½ tsp hot chili sauce
- Salt and black pepper to taste

Directions:

1. Place potatoes and enough water in a pot over medium heat and bring to a boil. Simmer for 15 minutes and drain. Let them cool. Cut them in halves and scoop out the pulp. Place the pulp in a bowl and mash it a bit with a fork. Add in the ricotta cheese, olive oil, garlic, chives, chili sauce, salt, and pepper. Mix to combine. Fill potato skins with the mixture.

2. Preheat oven to 360 F. Line a baking sheet with parchment paper. Place filled skins on the sheet and bake for 10 minutes.

Nutrition:

- Info Per Serving: Calories: 310;Fat: 10g;Protein: 9g;Carbs: 23g.

Salty Spicy Popcorn

Servings:6
Cooking Time:10 Minutes
Ingredients:

- 3 tbsp olive oil
- ¼ tsp garlic powder
- Salt and black pepper to taste
- ½ tsp dried thyme
- ½ tsp chili powder
- ½ tsp dried oregano
- 12 cups plain popped popcorn

Directions:

1. Warm the olive oil in a large pan over medium heat. Add the garlic powder, black pepper, salt, chili powder, thyme, and stir oregano until fragrant, 1 minute. Place the popcorn in a large bowl and drizzle with the infused oil over. Toss to coat.

Nutrition:

- Info Per Serving: Calories: 183;Fat: 12g;Protein: 3g;Carbs: 19g.

Tomato-cheese Toasts

Servings:4
Cooking Time:5 Minutes
Ingredients:

- 1 tomato, cubed
- 12 ounces cream cheese, soft
- ¼ cup mayonnaise
- 2 garlic clove, minced
- 1 red onion, chopped
- 2 tbsp lime juice
- 4 slices whole-wheat toast

Directions:

1. In a bowl, blend cream cheese, mayonnaise, garlic, onion, and lime juice until smooth. Spread the mixture onto the bread slices and top with the tomato cubes to serve.

Nutrition:

- Info Per Serving: Calories: 210;Fat: 7g;Protein: 5g;Carbs: 8g.

Fruit And Nut Chocolate Bark

Servings:2
Cooking Time: 2 Minutes
Ingredients:

- 2 tablespoons chopped nuts
- 3 ounces dark chocolate chips
- ¼ cup chopped dried fruit (blueberries, apricot, figs, prunes, or any combination of those)

Directions:

1. Line a sheet pan with parchment paper and s aside.
2. Add the nuts to a skillet over medium-high hea and toast for 60 seconds, or just fragrant. Set aside cool.
3. Put the chocolate chips in a microwave-safe gla bowl and microwave on High for 1 minute.
4. Stir the chocolate and allow any unmelted chips warm and melt. If desired, heat for an additional 20 30 seconds.
5. Transfer the chocolate to the prepared sheet pa Scatter the dried fruit and toasted nuts over th chocolate evenly and gently pat in so they stick.
6. Place the sheet pan in the refrigerator for at least hour to let the chocolate harden.
7. When ready, break into pieces and serve.

Nutrition:

- Info Per Serving: Calories: 285;Fat: 16.1g;Protei 4.0g;Carbs: 38.7g.

Home-style Trail Mix

Servings:4
Cooking Time:30 Minutes
Ingredients:

- 1 cup dried apricots, cut into thin strips
- 2 tbsp olive oil
- 1 cup pepitas
- 1 cup walnut halves
- 1 cup dried dates, chopped
- 1 cup golden raisins
- 1 cup raw almonds
- 1 tsp salt

Directions:

1. Preheat the oven to 310 F. Combine almond pepitas, dates, walnuts, apricots, and raisins in a bov Mix in olive oil and salt and toss to coat. Spread t mixture on a lined with parchment paper sheet, a bake for 30 minutes or until the fruits are slight browned. Let to cool before serving.

Nutrition:

- Info Per Serving: Calories: 267;Fat: 14g;Protei 7g;Carbs: 35g.

RECIPES INDEX

Made in the USA
Las Vegas, NV
21 December 2023

83412724R00063